Inside Formula 1

Father-and-son reflections from
seventy years of motorsport.
Jarno Trulli in the Toyota, 2006

INSIDE FORMULA 1

BEHIND-THE-SCENES PHOTOGRAPHY, 1950–2022

DANIEL REINHARD

SCHIFFER
PUBLISHING

4880 Lower Valley Road • Atglen, PA 19310

Contents

Foreword

Pictures Write History and Stories Create Pictures

We store events associated with strong emotions in our memory and can recall them later over and over again in image form. Over time, these images change in our memory—through the conscious or unconscious addition of elements. For example, we are sure that we saw a red car in front of a country estate under a bright blue sky. But the sun was covered by clouds at that time, and the car was far from being as noble and valuable as we remember it. A shot taken by a photographer is different.

The camera captures an ultrashort moment and turns it into a historical document. This shows our descendants how things really used to be.

The Other Book

It's every photographer's wish to one day present his pictures between two book covers. This is how umpteen thousand books about motorsport and, in particular, about Formula 1 have been written, but in the end, they are all very similar. The focus is on the sport with its results and events, but not on the creation of and the background behind individual images.

This book is completely different. For once, it doesn't list motorsport statistics such as world championship titles, winners, or losers, nor does it focus on the familiar series of top photos. Rather, it is intended to provide a behind-the-scenes look at motorsports from the perspective of two photographers, my father (Josef) and myself. We have been capturing the action for seventy years with a wide variety of camera systems—from black-and-white film to color slides to the digital world, from Juan-Manuel Fangio to Lewis Hamilton.

Our archive now contains several hundred thousand motorsport images. Digging through them was fun and thrilling at the same time. When I held one or the other picture in my hands and looked at it closely, the protagonists suddenly came to life and told me very special stories. The statements by two motorsport greats are very fitting. Walter Röhrl, for example, said of photographs: "For me, they are a great trip back in time." And Jackie Stewart said, "Photographs awaken all the great memories, not only the beautiful ones, but also all the sad ones."

Up Close and Personal

Journalists sit in the overheated or completely undercooled but always dry media center. There, they watch training sessions or races on various screens. At the same time, they are fed information from all sides. Only very rarely do they take the time to go to the racetrack. So they write about events that they haven't seen up close. What do you feel with your knee against the guardrail during the all-important qualifying lap by an Ayrton Senna in Monaco? How does it come across when the driver gets out of the car full of frustration or with great joy? How does a driver let his emotions run free after his first victory? And how does it feel to have to look death straight in the eye?

Unlike journalists, we photographers are always expected to stand right where the action is playing out with great drama. In order to get the really important pictures, we have to get up close and personal and sometimes even almost too close. Only at the very front is there THE PICTURE and also only in THE single, ultrashort MOMENT. Most of the time, only one picture emerges that is better than all the others. Only fractions of seconds later, it is all over and the situation cannot be repeated. The work of journalists is different: they can still describe the dramatic moment minutes later with a great deal of imagination—even if they never saw it with their own eyes.

It sounds crazy, but if we add up the exposure times of all 320 race shots shown in the book, this gives us a total working time of 66.658 seconds. My father and I spent seventy years working around the globe to achieve this all-important time. In the process, we always had only one thing in focus: the picture that would outlive us both and tell a story to our descendants.

Hans Herrmann and Sebastian Vettel discuss their respective eras in racing. We received a handwritten letter from each of them.

Lieber Dani,

was für eine Ehre einen Platz in Deinem Buch zu bekommen. Ich habe mich wirklich sehr darüber gefreut. Ich denke Du weißt, wie schade ich es finde, dass Du nicht mehr zu den Rennen kommst und Dich dort nicht mehr antreffen kann. Daher wünsche ich Dir auf diesem Wege alles Gute!

Ich habe unsere gemeinsame Zeit im Rennsport schätzen gelernt. Habe Dich als einen unglaublich offenen Menschen und leidenschaftliche Fotografen erlebt. Eine Leidenschaft für den Motorsport, die in Dir brennt, die Du stets offen, über Augen und Gesicht, ausstrahlst. Ich glaube diese Leidenschaft hat nicht nur mich berührt. Du hast damit viele Menschen inspiriert.

Ebenfalls hat es mich immer fasziniert Dir zuzuhören, als du erzählt hast, wie schnell die heutigen Autos sind und den richtigen Moment zu erwischen um die Rennwagen in voller Fahrt zu fotografieren. Zudem hattest Du noch das Glück die „früheren" Zeiten mitzuerleben. Deine Fotos, aber vor allem Deine Erzählungen aus dieser Zeit fand ich immer sehr spannend. In toller Erinnerung bleibe mir unsere Ausflüge, wie beispielsweise in Tokio. Was für ein Glück, dass Du, Profi wie du bist, immer Deine Kamera dabei hattest.

Alles Liebe, Dein Sebastian.

The start of the Brazilian Grand Prix on March 26, 1989. This was the last Formula 1 race held in Rio de Janeiro on the racetrack with the pleasant-sounding name Jacarepaguá. Here Ayrton Senna (McLaren) is sandwiched between Gerhard Berger (Ferrari) and Riccardo Patrese (Williams).

1 "I Saw You!"

Facial Expressions and the View through the Visor

After qualifying for the Spanish GP in 2002, Heinz-Harald Frentzen said to me, "You were standing in the left-hand curve at the end of the first chicane. I saw you!" My astonished reaction was "How could you have seen me there? How did you even have time to recognize me?" Frentzen's plausible explanation: "Dani, you were standing exactly at the point where I fixed my eyes on the next turn-in point. If you're standing right there, I can see and also recognize you. My gaze is directed at you for a brief moment. If you move even 2 meters (6.5 feet) to the left or right, you've left my point of focus," said Frentzen with a wink.

Button's Victory Look

It was glorious to watch how Jenson Button celebrated his first GP victory in the BAR-Honda at the 2006 Hungarian GP. I was able to shoot an incredibly expressive picture of him at just the right moment. The result speaks for itself, for Button's eyes say more than a thousand words. No journalist in the world could describe the moment better. Even through the viewfinder of the camera, the expression in his eyes was too short lived to be perceived. Only on the computer screen did the full power of the image become apparent.

Several photographs I was able to take of Andrea de Cesaris are very special. They are an expression of the incredible nervousness from which the Italian driver suffered. As a result, he was constantly turning his eyes in all directions—so much so that sometimes his pupils disappeared completely and only the whites of his eyes could be seen. Who knows? Perhaps his involuntary optical misfires were also responsible for the numerous accidents in his winless F1 career. Because of them, the Italian was nicknamed Andrea de "Crasharis."

Disinterest in the Car

Today, drivers are increasingly hiding from photographers. The halo safety device helps them do this. It takes away the view of the helmet, which in turn obscures the face. If the face is finally uncovered, dark sunglasses are certainly sitting on the driver's nose . . . how can emotionally charged portrait pictures be created in this way? At the end of the 1950s and the beginning of the 1960s, there was a well-known German photographer by the name of Dr. Benno Müller, a general practitioner by profession. His favorite hobby, however, was portrait photography. With his Leica and Hasselblad cameras, he photographed the drivers and only the drivers of the time. The cars did not interest him at all. Since training days were better suited for taking portraits, he usually left the track the day before the race. The beneficiary was my father, who often received the better accreditation from him. In the F1 camp, this saying circulated over time: "Dr. Benno Müller is leaving; now the race can begin!"

Jensen Button achieved his first Grand Prix win in Hungary in 2006.

Rain, stones, insects, wind: there were good reasons for the goggles worn by the early race car drivers.

Lucky Devil Massa, Unlucky Fellow Marko

At high speeds, the airstream would prevent pilots from seeing. Therefore, goggles and visors protect the drivers and ensure that they have a clear view whenever possible. Here, too, technological progress has been tremendous. Until the 1960s, racers often wore only a T-shirt and protected their heads and eyes with dust caps and goggles. Since 1968, the full-face helmet with visor has been standard equipment. But there is no such thing as complete protection. For the drivers of Monoposto race cars, there is no shield to protect them from rain, insects, the driving wind, or even foreign objects. At the French GP in 1972, for example, a stone ended the career of Dr. Helmut Marko of Graz. A stone thrown up by Ronnie Peterson pierced his visor and injured the BRM driver's eye so badly that it had to be replaced by a glass one. Felipe Massa was much luckier in qualifying for the 2009 Hungarian GP. A metal spring that had come loose from Barrichello's Brawn punctured the Brazilian's visor and caused him a severe head injury. During a lengthy operation, a bone splinter had to be removed from behind his left eye socket. Massa was lucky. He suffered no consequential damage and, unlike Marko, was able to continue his racing career.

John Surtees and Sebastian Vettel

Andrea de Cesaris, Sebastian Buemi, Juan Pablo Montoya, and Michael Schumacher

▼ Michael Schumacher checks the view through the visor.

2 Hollywood Says Hello

Niki Lauda: February 22, 1949–May 20, 2019

The year 1976 was a special one. The great duel for the world championship between the Briton James Hunt and Austrian Niki Lauda came to a head as the season progressed. Then disaster struck—the fiery crash involving Niki Lauda at the German Grand Prix on August 1 on the Bergwerk section of the track. The Austrian was seriously injured and for days was in intensive care, fighting for his life. Lauda's lungs had been seared by the fumes, and his face and hands were severely burned.

Back then, most racetracks were much longer, and there were only a few TV cameras along the track to capture images. As a result, only certain parts of the track could be seen on TV. The most extreme example was the Nürburgring, which was 22.835 kilometers (14.2 miles) long. When Lauda's fiery crash occurred, it was the last time that the full track was on the Formula 1 calendar. So it came as no surprise that there were no official TV pictures of the horrible crash. Instead, an amateur filmmaker managed to get the footage of a lifetime. He was standing in the right place and was able to capture the accident in its entirety with a simple Super 8 camera. After the film was developed, these images flickered across television sets around the world. Today, it would be completely different, since there is not a single section of the track that is not monitored by television cameras. The images of the burning Ferrari 312 T2 would be broadcast live to living rooms around the world.

Focus on Lauda

It bordered on a miracle. Niki Lauda missed just two Grand Prix races after his devastating accident. On September 12, just forty-two days after the crash at the Nürburgring, he climbed back into his Ferrari and started the Italian GP. The curious thing was that the Italian racing team had not believed that the Austrian would recover so quickly, and had already found a replacement for him in the form of Argentinean Carlos Reutemann, a replacement driver. So at Monza there were three Scuderia Ferrari cars in the starting grid. But Reutemann was of no interest to the numerous journalists who were present. Even world championship runner-up James Hunt was completely ignored by the media. They focused on Niki Lauda, who, however, was perfectly shielded. The aim of all the TV teams and photographers was to get a telling portrait of the Austrian revealing his flame-scarred face. Then all of a sudden it was there. The ultrashort moment when the view of the right side of Lauda's face was unobstructed. My father managed only a single exposure amid the crowd of photographers, but the result was an expressive picture! By the way, Lauda finished the race in an unbelievable fourth place and preserved his chance of winning the world championship title against the Englishman James Hunt.

The Hospital Instead of the World Championship Finale

The final race of the season, the Japanese Grand Prix, was held at Fuji Speedway for the first time. It was shaping up to be a Hitchcock finale. Lauda led the

"Little Red Riding Hood" Niki Lauda in a good mood

world championship standings with 68 points. Hunt was only 3 points behind. For my father and me, one thing was clear: we had to see this showdown, and we had to see it live on television! But the broadcast was no longer of interest to Swiss television—and we are Swiss—since Clay Regazzoni no longer had a chance of winning the title. It was different for ORF, the Austrian Broadcasting Corporation. But we could not receive it at our residence in Sachseln. So we had to act. My father bought a small portable television set, especially for this one race, which could be plugged into the car's cigarette lighter. On October 24, 1976, at the crack of dawn—the race started at 6 a.m. Central European time—we drove our red VW K70 into the mountains. With the TV set running on the hood, my father slowly steered the car through the wilderness until we were able to receive ORF to some extent in a clearing in the woods. The picture quality left something to be desired, but that was irrelevant. On the other hand, we could hear Heinz Prüller's commentary perfectly, which meant that we were live at this important event! At least that's what we thought—because the start was postponed again and again due to heavy rain. Finally, the time had come, and the drivers were sitting in their cars ready for the big showdown. But then the unbelievable happened. All of a sudden, a hunter drove past us on his Enduro Yamaha. He couldn't believe what he had seen: early in the morning, two people were watching TV in the wild with a mobile TV set on the hood of their car. To make sure that this was actually true, he turned around on his motocross bike. That's when it happened. He drove into the middle of a pile of wood that was next to the road, rolled over, and landed on his shoulder. With a broken collarbone, he lay moaning a few meters away from us. Instead of

watching the Formula 1 race, we took the injured hunter to the hospital. And thus, we missed Niki Lauda abandoning the race in the pouring rain with the following explanation: "My life is worth more than a title, no matter what the whole world thinks of me now." James Hunt became world champion despite our "absence."

With Lauda in the Movie Theater

Formula 1 wrote its perfect Hollywood script in 1976. The motion picture *Rush* was released in 2013. It was directed by the famous American director and Oscar winner Ron Howard. Niki Lauda was convincingly played by Daniel Brühl. I had built up a good friendship with the Austrian racing driver and motorsport expert over all the years. So I received a personal invitation from Lauda to the premiere of this cinematic event. Together with Michael Schmidt, Formula 1 editor at *Auto, Motor und Sport*, the makers of the film, and Niki's closest friends, we watched the film at the Stadtkino in Vienna's Künstlerhaus. For me, this was one of the very special experiences of my photography career.

At that time, the racetracks were not yet completely covered by TV cameras; consequently, there were no television pictures of the accident. But an amateur filmmaker managed to get the footage of a lifetime, capturing the entire accident with a simple Eumig Super 8 camera.

▲ Lauda at the Monaco Grand Prix in 1972, his first year in Formula 1

▶ The 1976 Monza Grand Prix: everyone was after a photo in which his fire-scarred face could be seen.

Niki Lauda twice: Daniel Brühl gave a convincing portrayal of the legend in the movie *Rush*.

3 The Racing Virus

How It All Began

I, Daniel Reinhard, born August 27, 1960, am a third-generation photographer. While my grandfather Josef (1901–1975) learned the craft autodidactically, my father, Josef, born on December 29, 1931, completed a professional apprenticeship in Lucerne. From then on, he devoted himself to reportage photography. As a photojournalist, he soon earned the nickname "Disaster Sepp," because his pictures in the daily newspapers often portrayed accidents or other disasters. He was infected by the racing virus at a young age. The Grand Prix racing cars from Mercedes-Benz held a special fascination for him.

As a teenager, Josef followed the races on the radio and especially in the cinema via the popular newsreels. They were a weekly compilation of film reports from all over the world on political, cultural, and even sporting events. My father had several friends who were just as crazy about motorsports as he was. Some of them later took part more or less successfully in regional races.

More and More Races

As a nineteen-year-old, my father was at the track for the Swiss GP in Bern in 1950. He was equipped with two cameras, a Leica M and a twin-lens Rolleiflex 6 × 6, which became my first camera in 1964. The fast cars fascinated him, and so he focused more and more on motorsport photography. Year after year, the number of races he attended grew. Bern was followed by Monza and Monaco and later by other tracks such as Reims, Hockenheim, Nürburgring, Zandvoort, Brands Hatch, and Dijon. Since the Swiss championship was still important at that time, he also photographed various national races.

Mercedes Mechanic

It's always been difficult to get the necessary accreditations for the races. Often, one needed a good network of contacts or a little vitamin B. Thanks to a good contact in the form of the then-Mercedes-Benz race director Alfred Neubauer, at the Swiss GP my father received an armband identifying him as a Mercedes mechanic. This, of course, gave him unrestricted access to the pit lane, and he was able to take photographs without being disturbed.

When his pictures began appearing more and more frequently in publications such as *Automobil-Revue* or *Powerslide*, it became easier for him to get the coveted accreditations. Sometimes even very small things, such as a large bar of Swiss chocolate, helped him reach his goal. The network among the photographers was also important. He maintained close friendships with his German professional colleagues Ulrich Schwab, Hans-Peter Seufert, and Jutta Fausel, and they helped each other out. My father was very busy at that time, even more so after his father's death in 1975. His primary occupation was photographing numerous subjects in central Switzerland every day, and he and his wife, Rosa, also ran a photo shop, which also sold stationery. Nevertheless, he remained faithful to racing until I could take over this work from him.

My own racing career came to an early end for financial reasons, but in 1975 I took second place in the soapbox race on the Polenstrasse in my Tyrrell racer wearing a Clark helmet.

A dream came true at Le Luc in 2020, when I was able to drive a Formula 1 car.

Help from Doctor Ferrari

In the summer of 1960, my father attended the test drives in Monza. My mother, who was very pregnant, was also there. The loud engine noise must have bothered me a bit, and I passed on my prenatal discomfort to my mother. In short, the contractions started and got stronger and stronger. On the drive back from Monza, it became clear that things could not continue without urgent medical assistance. Although my father is rather helpless in such situations, he headed for a phone booth in Lugano and began to look in the telephone directory for a doctor. Under the letter "F," he came across the name "Doctor of Medicine Ferrari." This immediately seemed to him to be the right doctor. And lo and behold, Dottore Ferrari brought the strong contractions to a halt, and we were able to continue our journey home.

School Psychologist

I came into the world and grew up with gasoline in my blood. Always around me was my photographer father, who mainly took pictures of cars. That wasn't always an advantage. In 1967, my kindergarten teacher, a nun, thought that there was something wrong with my behavior. She sent me to the school psychologist because of the pictures I drew. After an extensive therapy session, he gave the all-clear. It turned out that all the dark pictures I was drawing were nothing out of the ordinary. I had merely taken the prints made by my father, who photographed in black and white and which I admired after the race weekends, as a model for my drawings. Consequently, it was logical that I painted only with black paint and that the subjects consisted of racetracks and racing cars, sometimes even with just three wheels. Or to put it another way: for me, there were no colors at all back then. My world of images corresponded to my father's black-and-white photographs. By the way, even years later in high school, I found drawing race cars in class much more exciting than following the boring Latin lessons.

The Accident

I experienced my first car race in 1965 at the tender age of five. It was a mountain race in central Switzerland

and led from Grafenort up to the monastery village of Engelberg. My father, Josef, placed me in the spectator area at the first hairpin curve and then went to the photographer's area. From there, I was always in his field of vision. Before long, Werner Biedermann from Zurich braked his beautiful Ferrari 250 LM and tumbled down the slope into the depths, and I immediately ran right across the track to my father so that I could see exactly what had happened. This did not go down at all well with the commissioners. My father got a reprimand, and he put me through the wringer. Fortunately, the driver was not injured. But he was so shocked by the accident that he immediately ended his racing career. In me, however, the crash sparked racing fever.

I sat in the grandstand for the first time with my mother on October 13, 1968, at a Formula 2 race at Hockenheim. I still remember the serious accident involving a motorcycle-sidecar at the entrance to the Motodrom. And I can recall at any time the pictures of Jo Siffert in the white Lola T102-BMW M12, as well as those of the gigantic traffic jam from the press parking lot all the way to the highway. The grandstand we were sitting on back then had to make way for the new Porsche Experience Center in 2019.

Taken Short

I experienced my first Formula 1 Grand Prix, still in the stands, in Monaco in 1972. My father had traveled with my mother and me to Monte Carlo for a few days to take in this annual motorsport event. However, since my mother wasn't really interested in racing and grandstand seats were becoming expensive even back then, at the age of twelve I was allowed to watch the race alone. Before the start, my father took me to my seat on the start-finish straight and told me to stay there until he came back to pick me up. Weather-wise, however, it was a terrible day, and it started to rain more and more. I can still remember that after the race started, I suddenly felt the urge to urinate. But I had no idea where the toilet was. Moreover, I was afraid that I would not be able to find my way back to my grandstand seat. Since I didn't speak a word of French either, and I realized that there was almost no one who could help me, I peed in my pants during the race. No one noticed, because the rain had completely soaked all the spectators anyway.

Little Daniel with the Rolleiflex 6 x 6, signed by Dan "Daniel" Gurney

This drawing, all in black, caused me to be sent to the school psychologist.

Swiss Victory in the First Race

In 1973, I was allowed to accompany my father to the 1,000-kilometer (621-mile) race at Monza for the first time. I really wanted to take my own pictures there. To ready myself for this several days beforehand, I stood at the crest of our village drive-through and photographed passing passenger cars. Of course, their speed wasn't comparable to that of the racing cars at Monza. But I got a feel for how to photograph moving cars.

From 1976 to 1978, I was already photographing various races in the Swiss championship series without my father's supervision. Since I did not yet have a driver's license, I traveled to various races with Thomas Suter, who at that time wrote for the

My first attempts at photographing moving objects. Traffic passing through Sachseln, 1973.

magazine *Motorsport Aktuell* (*Current Motorsport*), which was created from *Powerslide*. During the same period, I also developed a very close friendship with my professional colleague Jimmy (Jean-Pierre) Froidevaux (deceased on July 26, 2019, just short of his seventy-fifth birthday). I made my Formula 1 debut at Silverstone on July 14, 1979, without the support of my father. Located in the county of Northamptonshire, the potholed circuit was not at all popular with photographers. The photo areas were too far away from the track. Therefore, many photographers did not bother to make the trip there. I planned to attend the race during an Interrail trip from London to Scotland and had no idea what to expect. In the absence of most Swiss motorsport journalists, Clay Regazzoni won the race ahead of René Arnoux and Jean-Pierre Jarier. This was the Swiss driver's first victory for the British Williams team. For me, it was an absolute stroke of luck. I was in the right place at the right time. While I continued my journey to Scotland, Adriano Cimarosti, sports editor of *Automobil-Revue*, took my photographs back to Switzerland on the next scheduled flight. There they found their way straight into various newspapers.

After Vienna, Self-Employment

During my training in Vienna, I continued pursuing motorsport photography as intensively as possible. I attended various races in Austria and the neighboring countries and made contact with the magazine *Auto-Revue*. The latter printed my regional (rally-cross in Melk) and international (European Touring Car Championship in Brno) pictures. Axel Höfer, already an editorial veteran at that time, became my reference person. This resulted in a friendship that we still maintain today.

In the summer of 1984, I completed my studies in Vienna. I stayed in the Austrian capital for another year and became a photo assistant at Studio 2 with Fred Peer. Of course, I accepted the job only on the condition that I could continue to attend some races. A close friendship also developed with Fred. In 1986, I returned to Switzerland and started my own business.

1972 Monaco Grand Prix. Niki Lauda at the wheel of the March ahead of eventual victor Jean-Pierre Beltoise in the BRM.

Close friendship among professional colleagues: Uli Schwab, HP Seufert, and my father (wearing the straw hat). The photo was taken by Jutta Fausel, the fourth member of the team.

Issue 18 of *Auto, Motor und Sport* appeared on my birthday, August 27, 1960. I began working for this great magazine twenty-seven years later.

Who would have believed the story about the deer from a nineteen-year-old in a fast Alfasud?

◀ The Grafenort-Engelberg mountain race in 1965 was my first contact with the racing scene. Werner Biedermann's wrecked Ferrari 250 LM.

Josef Reinhard with his first automobile, a Goggomobil, with Fredi Baumann, a friend from his youth, in the Cooper racecar after a test drive, of course on a public road

4 Mercedes-Benz Seeks Protection

The First Documents

Our first photos of a racing car were taken in 1946. They are also linked to an exciting story.

Mercedes-Benz brought its Grand Prix cars to Switzerland shortly before the start of the Second World War to safeguard them. They were hidden behind a protective wall in the cellar of the Mercedes-Benz branch in Schlieren near Zurich. At that time, my grandfather maintained a friendly relationship with Helmut Hirzel, the head of the then Mercedes-Benz Schweiz AG. That's why he got the information that the racing cars were to be taken out of hiding for a function test shortly after the end of the war. The reason: the German automaker was considering entering one of these cars in the Indy 500, the first officially announced race. As you can see in the pictures, the Mercedes-Benz W165 with its 1.5-liter V8 engine, which had been specially developed for the Tripoli Grand Prix of May 7, 1939, is running in the exit of the underground garage. Much to the excitement of my then-fifteen-year-old father, German racing driver Rudolf Caracciola was present at this function test. He took a few rare medium-format photo documents with his Rolleiflex.

However, Mercedes-Benz was refused entry for its race cars into the USA. Caracciola, therefore, had to train for the Indy 500 with an American Marmon. However, he did not get far. At high speed, a bird flew into his face. Caracciola was forced to withdraw from the race.

In 1952, "Karatsch," who had been living in Lugano with Swiss citizenship since 1946, had a serious accident in a 300 SLR. He collided with a tree during the sports car race on the occasion of the Swiss GP in Bern and was pulled from the car with a triple fracture of the lower leg. A great racing career thus came to an end. Caracciola died in Kassel in 1959.

The Mercedes-Benz W165 Silberpfeil (Silver Arrow) during a test run at Schlieren near Zurich in 1946

Rudolf Caracciola sends the
Mercedes-Benz 300SLR flying
through the gravel plant on the
Bremgartenring circuit.

The end of a great career. Two Swiss soldiers carry the badly injured Caracciola away after his collision with a tree.

HANS HERRMANN

STUTTGART-O
HAUPTSTÄTTERSTR. 91
TELEFON 07049 40222

9. Aug. 55.

Worast. 47

Lieber Herr Reinhard!

Zuerst möchte ich mich für Ihren lb.
Brief nebst Bildern herzlichst be-
danken.
Mich zu entschuldigen, für das lange
Ausbleiben meiner Antwort, getraue
ich mich kaum mehr, den dann ist
es schon zu lange her. Aber ich habe
Sie deshalb nicht vergessen.

Mit meinem Gesundheitszustand bin
ich sehr zufrieden, u. glaube bis in 2
Monaten wieder ganz hergestellt zu sein,
nur sind bis dahin leider auch fast
schon alle Rennen gelaufen u. kann so.
mit nur auf Mexico mit Bestimmtheit
rechnen. Bin deshalb aber nicht unzu-
frieden, den ich muss froh sein, das

Alles noch einmal gut abgelaufen ist

In der Hoffnung, dass es
auch Ihnen gut geht, grüsst Sie
Ihr
Hans Herrmann

For many years, the letter was the most important medium of communication. Communication was made easier with the introduction of the fax in the late 1970s. This was later followed by email and, beginning in 1992, text messaging. Today, most information exchanges take place on social media platforms. They make it possible to share text messages, pictures, and videos in any form. At present, we can hardly imagine what it was like when the letter was the principal communications medium. Written by hand or on a typewriter, with as few errors as possible to avoid embarrassment, it was sent from A to B with the appropriate stamp. It often took weeks for the recipient to reply.

Hans Hermann's Letter from 1955

As soon as the pictures from a race were developed, the photographer often sent a few prints to the racers by mail. This was only good manners and was practiced by my father, Josef. Exactly such an exchange of letters took place in 1955 between my father and Mercedes Formula 1 driver Hans Herrmann from Stuttgart.

Fortunately, my father meticulously kept all the letters. When I met Herrmann in 2018 on the occasion of an interview for *Auto, Motor und Sport* in Stuttgart, I presented him with the letter. His reaction touched me. "Look at this; this is incredible!" he said. And as an allusion to the highly commercialized Formula 1 of today, he said, "Which F1 driver today would still write back personally to a photographer and even apologize for the long wait?" After a moment's thought, he added, "I had an accident in Monte Carlo at the time, where my Mercedes crashed into the stone balustrade at the Massenet corner with the brakes locked. I remember very well that I wrote the letter after being hospitalized." With tears in his eyes, he read through sentence after sentence of the letter and at the end said, "That you still have this document. That's just sensational."

Hans Herrmann reading the letter that he wrote sixty-three years earlier

Vettel, the Exception to the Rule

There are many other great racing drivers who took the time to correspond with people like my father back then. Our family archives contain letters from John Surtees, Stirling Moss, Hermann Lang, and Louis Chiron, and even Mercedes race director Alfred Neubauer wasn't above writing lengthy letters. Coming back to Hans Herrmann's statement about which F1 driver today would take the time to write back personally to a photographer, I can't think of many names.

But as always, there is an exception to the rule. And that exception is four-time world champion Sebastian Vettel (see the foreword)!

5 Banking Fascination

The Legendary Curves at Monza and the AVUS Circuit

Photographers love action. This usually takes place in curves. Two legendary banked curves produce special photographs. Racing drivers are able to take them at very high speeds, but they pose special challenges to photographers.

The measure of all things was the two really high banked curves at Monza and on the AVUS circuit. The steep-banked curve on the AVUS was created in 1937 to increase the lap speed of the racetrack, which is located southwest of Berlin. For this purpose, bricks were used to convert the north curve into a 43.6-degree steep curve with a significantly smaller radius. In 1967, the banked curve was removed for safety reasons.

In 1954, extensive construction work was carried out at Monza, turning the ultrafast oval circuit with its two 875-meter (0.54-mile) straightaways into a normal racetrack. This resulted in the creation of two 320-meter-long (1,050-foot) and up to 80 percent banked curves, which permitted tremendous speeds. The 10-kilometer (6.2-mile) track, including the oval, was part of Formula 1 racing in 1955, 1956, 1960, and 1961. In 1957 and 1958, the oval was also the scene of a unique competition: in the Race of Two Worlds, also called "Monzanapolis," the heroes of the Indy 500 raced against drivers from Europe.

The two Porsche 908 LH race cars driven by Siffert/Redman and Herrmann/Ahrens, followed by three Ford GT 40s during the 1,000-km race in 1969

◄ An attraction for fans, a major challenge for the drivers, and especially for the cars

39

▶ The 1,000-km race at Monza in 1967. Mike Spence and Phil Hill in the sensational Chaparral 2F leading the eventual victor, the Ferrari 330 P4 driven by Lorenzo Bandini and Chris Amon.

Vitamin B

For photographers, the steep banked curves meant extra work. Only a few positions were suitable for the right camera angle, and these were highly coveted. So anyone who wanted to get an optimal spot at Monza needed a lot of vitamin B—especially if they weren't Italian.

In 1965, the oval at Monza was used by sports prototypes only for the 1,000-kilometer (621-mile) race. As these cars also became faster and faster, the two steeply banked walls were abandoned. They have not been used since 1970. In the meantime, they have been extensively renovated and can again be used for advertising purposes and film and photo shoots.

The Waving Jo Siffert

My father was given several opportunities to take pictures from one of the towers on the steep banked track into the bend during the 1,000-kilometer (621-mile) races. This resulted in unique documents that are still fascinating today. But it wasn't easy to capture the action of the race cars and the steepness of the curve in the same picture. The photographer's position and focal length had to be right, and the driver had to take the curve in just the right place. So in 1968, my father asked the racing driver Jo Siffert to drive his Porsche 908LH past, as high up in the curve as possible. He did this for a few laps, each time waving to him. A typical reaction from Jo "Seppi" Siffert. He was always ready to help and was pleased to do so.

For a long time, they seemed to be out, but suddenly banked curves are again being built, like the one at Zandvoort.

The decay was stopped and both banked curves were renovated. They are relics of the fascinating history of motorsport.

The banked curve at Monza prior to
renovation, a cultural asset with patina

▶ The two Ferrari 275 P2s in formation during the
1,000-km race at Monza on April 25, 1965

► The banked curve from the spectator's perspective. The Ferrari 312P driven by Mario Andretti and Chris Amon passing the Porsche 908 of Jo Siffert / Brian Redman on the outside.

▼▼ The Caracciola Carousel is one of the most fascinating photo spots in the green hell. When Nick Heidfeld drove round the Nordschleife in the BMW Sauber F1.06 on April 28, 2007, thirty years had passed since the last F1 appearance on this dreaded track. A helicopter was on standby for team manager Beat Zehnder, who carried a radio for air-ground communication, and me as photographer to document Nick's legendary drive. But unfortunately, it turned out that the driver was not familiar with the track. Consequently, he lost his way in the race car and was already flying toward Belgium before I realized his mistake and was able to show him the way. At the end of the three laps, we waited in the air for his arrival at the finish line, but the hovering helicopter was drifting backward very slowly, and if Beat had not suddenly and miraculously spotted the power pole and the lines behind us, these lines would probably never have been written.

In 1961, my father absolutely had to document the building of the Berlin Wall, which divided Berlin into two parts. Naturally, this included a photo of the north corner of the AVUS circuit. The slide was framed between glass and, as a result, suffered some ill effects over the years. It was intentionally not retouched for presentation here. The writing on the wall says, "There is only ONE Berlin!"

6 Entry into F1 Sponsorship

The Middle Finger

Emotions can be perfectly captured in pictures. A racing driver doesn't always express joy. Often, it's also frustration and anger. For example, at the 1995 Australian GP in Adelaide, Heinz-Harald Frentzen in the Sauber "gave the finger" to his rival Mark Blundell in the McLaren after a traffic jam. The action was perfectly documented by the onboard camera. I immediately had the idea for a new sponsorship. I procured a pair of new gloves from Heinz-Harald Frentzen and had "Foto Reinhard " professionally embroidered on the right middle finger. Before the next race, I gave him back the gloves with the explanation, "I will give you a hundred francs per TV second." Heinz-Harald thought it was a funny idea. But I never had to pay anything for the sponsorship.

Vettel's Middle Finger

Of course, the middle finger was still used frequently, but mostly purely for fun, as in the case of Bernie Ecclestone or Sebastian Vettel. Vettel spotted me at the side of the track during the "Driver's Parade" at the French GP in Magny-Cours in 2008 and exchanged his raised thumb for the middle finger for a very brief moment. When he realized that there were other photographers at the side of the track, he was embarrassed by what he had done. Vettel was lucky. No other photographer caught the moment or passed the image on to the media. This example impressively shows that drivers, photographers, and journalists are often a close-knit group, sticking together, and are also up for a bit of fun. In the past more often than today, of course.

By the way: the pictures presented here have never been published before.

A sponsorship that was never used: Heinz-Harald Frentzen's glove

◀ Bernie Ecclestone, the "Great Zampano" of Formula 1, gives the photographer the middle finger.

7 Hill Climbers

Mountain Races with Formula 1 Stars

In the past, circuit races weren't the only thing that set the standard in motorsports. Hill climbing races were just as popular. The European mountain championship reached its peak between 1957 and 1969, with manufacturers even developing their own mountain racing cars, often referred to as paper airplanes because of their lightness. These included, for example, the Porsche 909 Bergspyder (mountain spider), which weighed a mere 430 kg (948 lbs.) and was powered by a 275-hp engine. Three Swiss drivers won the European mountain championship title: Zurich's Willy Peter Daetwyler (1957, Maserati 200 SI), Heini Walter (1960 and 1961, Porsche 718 RSK and RS 60), and Dr. Peter Schetty (1969, Ferrari 212 E Montagna). Daetwyler, however, had to fight hard for the title in 1957 against Wolfgang Count Berghe von Trips, who was coming on in his Porsche at the end of the season.

The following year, Trips took his revenge, ushering in Porsche's long period of domination. The Stuttgart-based company dominated in 1959, 1963, and 1964 with Edgar Barth, 1960 and 1961 with Heini Walter, and 1966 to 1968 with Gerhard Mitter. In this short period, they took the title no fewer than eight times. Ferrari won the championship in 1962 and 1965 with Ludovico Scarfiotti and in 1969 with Peter Schetty.

F1 on the Mountain

Mountain races attracted many visitors at that time. No wonder. Time and again, Formula 1 drivers also took part. This was also the case at various races for the European Mountain Championship in Switzerland. In 1964, Jack Brabham of Australia took to the starting line in Sierre-Montana in his Brabham. A year later, Briton Jim Clark took part in the St. Ursanne–Les Rangiers Hillclimb race in the asymmetrical Lotus 38 with which he had won the Indianapolis 500 just a few weeks earlier. In 1968, Switzerland's Jo Siffert also competed there in a Lotus 49-Ford as the newly crowned winner of the England Grand Prix and took the victory. Clay Regazzoni swapped the steering wheel of his Formula 1 Ensign for that of a Formula 2 March BMW for one race in 1977 and was a star guest and crowd magnet at the St. Peterzell–Hemberg hill climb.

Difficult Conditions

For us photographers, hill climbs are not easy to manage logistically. Unlike circuit races, we get to see the drivers only once, so every shot has to be perfect. That's why the training sessions are just as important for our work as the race. Since there is always a demand for pictures of the atmosphere at the start of the race, as well as action shots from the track, we have to decide early on which subject we want to photograph in practice or during the race. The day of the race guarantees more-attractive pictures of the start because the drivers are surrounded by a crowd of spectators. On the other hand, there is not enough time to take pictures along

There's no racing in Indianapolis when it rains. Here, Jim Clark tackles the St. Ursanne–Les Rangiers hill climb in the pouring rain in the Indy Lotus 38 with its asymmetric suspension in 1965, to the great enthusiasm of the fans.

the track in the same race. Stupid only if the weather does not cooperate. What photographer could, with a clear conscience, offer his customers an action picture of the winner on a wet track, which he shot during training—even though the race took place the following day in bright sunshine. Because of these conditions, only a few pictures were taken at hill climbs. So my father sometimes came home with just three rolls of exposed film with twelve shots each.

Advertising Jobs

To make matters worse, a race weekend wasn't just about taking pictures for newspapers and magazines. Companies frequently ordered photos for use in advertising. For example, at Siffert's start at the St. Ursanne–Les Rangiers hill climb in 1968, the tire company Firestone insisted that my father take a picture of the logo hanging above the Formula 1 Lotus as the race started.

> Thirty-six shots—and no more; an excellent result in the conditions that prevailed in a mountain race

At that time, the commercialization of racing was only in its infancy. So advertising shots were possible that are unthinkable today. My father received one of these special orders from Wander AG in 1971 for the Ollon-Villars mountain race. The company wanted to associate the popular Swiss cocoa drink Ovomaltine with racing in order to increase sales. The strange thing about this was that Wander had no contract with either the organizer or any of the racers. The staging in the pre-start zone of the race took place as follows: Two representatives of Wander AG strutted around the race cars with thermos flasks and served the waiting pilots a cup of hot Ovaltine. My father had to record this in pictures, and Wander produced an advertising poster from it practically free of charge with the slogan "Ovomaltine—To Perform Better." Today, the manufacturer of the cocoa drink would certainly have to shell out a seven-figure sum. This would be the responsibility of the drivers' management, which, together with lawyers, would probably spend weeks drawing up a contract dozens of pages thick.

◀ Peter Bauer in the McLaren during the 1969 Campo-Blenio-Luzzone hill climb in the canton of Ticino (Tessin). The parc-fermé (a secure area at a circuit where cars are checked over for legality and safety) was located on the Luzzone dam, which was completed in 1963.

A picture with personal dedication on the reverse from Willy Peter Daetwyler, the 1957 European hill climbing champion. Here he is seen with his Ferrari 750 Monza, taken on May 29, 1955, at the Nürburgring.

Mit dem Großen Preis von Italien in Monza ging die diesjährige «Grand-Prix»-Saison auf dem europäischen Kontinent zu Ende. Wenn nun die Piloten mit ihren Formel-1-Boliden nach Übersee dislozieren, so befindet sich unter ihnen bereits der Weltmeister des Jahres 1971. Seit dem achten Lauf der Fahrer-Weltmeisterschaft, dem Großen Preis von Österreich in Zeltweg, kennt man ihn: Jackie Stewart, den spleenigen Schotten. – Mit Siegen in den Grand Prix von Spanien (Barcelona), Monaco (Monte Carlo), Frankreich (Le Castellet), England (Silverstone) und Deutschland (Nürburgring) sowie einer Klassierung in Kyalami (GP von Südafrika) sicherte er sich ein so großes Punktetotal, daß ihn kein Konkurrent mehr entthronen kann. – Zusammen mit dem jungen Franzosen François Cevert (links) freut sich Jackie Stewart (auf unserm Bild rechts) über den Erfolg auf dem Nürburgring.

Ovomaltine
um mehr zu leisten

Einer wurde gejagt!

Dank ihres Top-Fahrers Jackie Stewart liegt Ford auch im Markenklassement an erster Stelle. Die Tyrell-Ford-V8-Maschine und ihr weltmeisterlicher Pilot bildeten das imponierendste Gespann der diesjährigen «Grand-Prix»-Saison.

Sie prägten
die Rennsaison 1971

Schöne Frauen und heiße Motoren sind eng mit dem Rennsport verbunden. Sowohl Fahrer wie Maschinen brauchen immer wieder «Unterstützung», die einen durch hübsche Holde, die andern durch fachmännische Hände.

Ovomaltine
um mehr zu leisten

Auch sie gehören zur Gilde der etablierten Formel-1-Fahrer: Der Belgier Jacky Ickx (oben, mit Gattin) galt als gefährlichster Gegner von Namensvetter Stewart; der Deutsche Rolf Stommelen (rechts) wartet immer noch auf den ersten Großerfolg.

Autorennfahrer wissen genau, daß OVOMALTINE leistungsfähig macht. An nationalen Rennen wird dieses Aufbaugetränk besonders geschätzt. Claude Haldi (oben) und Arthur Blank (unten) bewiesen dies anläßlich des Bergrennens Ollon-Villars.

Die Schweiz, als Land ohne Rundstreckenrennen, gehört zu den führenden Nationen in der Sparte der schnellsten Motoren. Mit Jo Siffert stellt sie sogar einen der diesjährigen GP-Sieger. Im Großen Preis von Österreich gelang dem Fribourger der zweite «grand coup» in seiner Karriere als Formel-1-Pilot.

Sie prägten die Rennsaison 1971, von links: Weltmeister Jackie Stewart und sein Tyrell-Ford; der Schweizer Clay Regazzoni mit drei GP-Klassierungen und Ferrari-Rennleiter Dr. Peter Schetty, der eben einen Einsatz seines Tessiner Schützlings vorbereitet.

Three shots (Dr. Peter Schetty, Roland Salomon, and Silvio Moser) from the international motorsport Ovomaltine campaign, with the end product

▲ Il grande (the great) Ludovico Scarfiotti sitting on his Ferarri Dino Spyder

▶▲ The two Porsche 910 Bergspyder (Mountain Spyders) of Rolf Stommelen and Gerhard Mitter at the starting line at Ollon in 1967

▶▼ Incredible numbers of spectators around the Holzschlägermatte corner during the 1959 Schauinsland Hill Climb

▲▲ Clay Regazzoni with Markus Hotz at the Hemberg Hill Climb in 1978

▲▲ Fiat Abarth during the Eigental Hill Climb in Lucerne

▲ Heini Walter in the Porsche 550 Spyder at the Mitholz-Kandersteg Hill Climb in 1958

▲ Dr. Peter Schetty in the Ferarri 212 Montagna at Ollon-Villars Hill Climb in 1969

Willy Peter Daetwyler in the Ferarri
750 Monza on the old St. Ursanne-
Les-Rangiers Hill Climb course on
September 9, 1955.

Swiss national hero Seppi Siffert in his Lotus 49 at the starting line at St. Ursanne in 1968

Rolf Stommelen in his Porsche 910
Bergspyder during the Ollon-Villars
Hill Climb in 1967

This shocking moment resulted in a spectacular photo for Josef Reinhard. Charles Ramu-Caccia's out-of-control Alfa Romeo TZ slams into the barrier behind the photographer, still in focus.

From the Racetrack to the Printing House

Huge Logistical Effort for a Few Pictures

Formula 1 works only thanks to masterpieces of logistics. Not only the racing cars, but also all the equipment, have to be transported from racetrack to racetrack. We photographers are also constantly on the move. In the past, hara-kiri exercises were often necessary to ensure that the pictures found their way from the racetrack via the photo lab to the newspapers and magazines on time. Since digitalization, our work has become much easier.

Midnight Deadline

In the era of analog photography, every minute was precious. For my father and me, the question at that time was this: When did we have to leave the racetrack so that we had enough time at home to develop the pictures? So we calculated backward. At five o'clock on Monday morning, we had to hand over the prints in 13 × 18 format to the railroad mail car so that they would arrive at *Automobil Revue* in Bern and *Powerslide* (now *Motorsport Aktuell*) in Zurich on time. It took us about five hours to develop the films, select the pictures, and drive to Lucerne. Thus, midnight was always our deadline for returning after a race weekend.

This tight schedule was possible only because we had our own postmark. We were therefore allowed to weigh, stamp, and postmark the envelopes containing the photos ourselves at home. Without this not-quite-official assistance from the post office, our motorsport pictures would never have reached the editorial offices on time.

The most extreme example was the 1986 Portuguese GP at Estoril. Since there was no suitable direct flight from Lisbon to Zurich, I had to improvise. So I left the race on Sunday afternoon after just five laps. From the racetrack, I took a rental car to Lisbon, flew to Lyon, got into the car I had left at the airport on Thursday, and traveled back to Sachseln. I arrived home just in time at 11:55 p.m. and immediately went to the photo lab.

From 1987 on, things got easier for me. As an employee of *Sport Auto and Auto, Motor und Sport*, I was able to give the exposed color slide films to editor Michael Schmidt. Depending on the editorial deadline, he had them developed either on Sunday night or early Monday morning in Stuttgart. Afterward, the editors made the image selection, and I picked up the remaining slides on Tuesday. This procedure worked well for the races in Europe.

Overseas Air Freight

When shipping from overseas, I very often had to work with air freight. In each case, I dropped off the package containing the films at the freight office of the desired airline, and a volunteer from Motorpresse picked it up at the airport in Frankfurt. To spread out the risk, I sent one package from each day of practice. At the Japanese Grand Prix at Suzuka, it went like this: Practice ended at 2 p.m. on Friday. A scooter immediately took me to Shirokko station, where I boarded the prebooked train shortly before 3 p.m. Three hours later, I arrived in Osaka and took a cab to the airport to check in the films at the cargo office. I then traveled back to Suzuka, arriving at the hotel at 11:30 p.m. On Saturday, the procedure was repeated. On Monday after the race, I flew home and took the pictures of the race back to Frankfurt in person.

As early as the 1970s, my father had sent undeveloped black-and-white film from South Africa to Switzerland. Once, the normally round containers arrived at our house completely flat. A heavy object had squashed the bag they were in. Fortunately, the films were from Kodak (PlusX and TriX-Pan) and not from Ilford (FP4 and HP5), because the Americans welded their containers, while Ilford just pressed the lids on. The film stock had not been exposed to light and was therefore still usable.

How times change. An image showing a simple paddock at the 1971 Formula 2 race in Vallelunga.

Birds Chirping at Night

Step by step, technical innovations brought with them simpler ways of working. My friend Jimmy Froidevaux often used the latest innovations to get his pictures to the editors faster than most colleagues.

At the end of the 1980s, he bought a picture fax machine for a lot of money. But this box, the size of a modern printer, could not transfer negatives or slides, only finished paper pictures. I often shared a hotel room with Jimmy. We converted the bathroom into a darkroom, where he developed the black-and-white film. In the suitcase, we had a detachable enlarger, and we used it to print the pictures. Then we spent hours transmitting them over the telephone network to Europe. The device chirped like a flock of wild birds during transmission. We had to take turns getting up throughout the night to send the next picture. Due to the hours-long telephone connection to Europe, the long-distance costs increased immeasurably and far exceeded the overnight costs.

When digitization arrived at the turn of the millennium, it was a massive relief for us photographers. Pictures could be sent to the editorial office by computer immediately after the training sessions and the race. This also increased the hectic pace. In the analog age, the pictures of a race were available only days later, whereas today they are on the internet before the race is over.

70 Years of Formula 1

In all my years as a motorsport photographer, countless working days came together. My 553 Formula 1 races, each of which included two training days, alone add up to over four and a half years spent on racetracks. That's not counting the many test days and travel days. In total, my father and I took photos on forty different Grand Prix circuits over our combined seventy years, spread over twenty-seven countries around the globe.

Added to this are the destinations of other racing series, such as the European Touring Car Championship, the IndyCar Series, the World Sports Car Championship, the DRM (German Racing Championship), DTM (German Touring Car Masters), and even Formula E.

Drugs in the Luggage

With such a large amount of travel, every now and then something went wrong. My father had really bad luck only once. On the return trip from the Monaco GP in 1974, an engine fire on a Swissair plane in Nice caused the plane to abort its takeoff. The result was an extra night in France. At least Swissair covered part of the loss of earnings at that time.

My most unnerving experience was on the return flight from the GP Holland in Zandvoort in 1979. The security agent in Amsterdam actually wanted to open my exposed film containers to make sure that there were no drugs in them. Of course, I didn't agree at all and a heated discussion ensued. Only after I presented the official with my press pass from the race and opened two canisters containing unexposed film did he let me pass.

Almost Stranded

I was lucky in 2010 when the Icelandic volcano Eyjafjallajökull erupted and virtually paralyzed all air traffic in northern and central Europe. I was at the Chinese Grand Prix in Shanghai when all regular European flights were canceled. On Sunday evening after the race, I received a call from Michael Schmidt in a sky bar high above Shanghai. "Dani, we have to go to the airport immediately. There is a plane chartered by Mercedes to fly to Munich at three o'clock." We left immediately. But at check-in we were told that the charter would not be flying. Instead, a Swiss plane was ready at short notice to fly its European passengers back at 7:00. My good luck: since in the middle of the night, many passengers were unaware of the short-notice return flight, I was able to get one of the last seats. My colleague Mathias Brunner was less fortunate, since he did not come to the airport with us and decided to fly via Kuala Lumpur. It took him a whole week to get home.

With Just Two Lenses

Over the past forty years, I have photographed more than a thousand motorsport events. Only once did I have to pass. In 1990, I tore the cruciate ligament in my right knee while skiing in St. Moritz. I had to undergo surgery, and the San Marino GP in Imola took place without me. I missed Riccardo Patrese's

▲▲ 1957 Italian GP at Monza. Two factory Maserati 250F race cars on an open truck waiting for their journey home.

▲▲ From the days when simple, private modes of transport were still possible. A Formula Junior car at the Solitude Grand Prix in 1961.

▲ Even the Formula 1 crews lived simply. Here is the Rob Walker team at the Spanish GP in Barcelona in 1969.

▲ After a tough 12-hour race, in the Reims pit lane the Ferrari 250LMs are prepared for the journey home.

victory but was back in Monaco two weeks later with the help of a special homemade boot and a crutch. My freedom of movement was considerably restricted and my equipment reduced to a minimum, just two lenses with different focal lengths. But the results were amazing. The example made it clear to me that it is (sometimes) better to focus on the essentials.

The Short End of the Stick

In all those years, I also had a few run-ins with the authorities. In 1982, on my way back from Le Mans, the French police were waiting for me at the highway toll booth in Belfort. They politely congratulated me on having the fastest time of the day (210 kph in my Alfetta GTV6). Then the friendliness was over. To be allowed to drive on at all, I had to pay two hundred francs on the spot. Eight hundred were added after the later court hearing. At least I didn't have to surrender my driver's license.

However, I was really harassed in 1990. I was on my way to Le Castellet for the Sauber-Mercedes C11 test and wanted to cross the border in Geneva. The customs officer demanded a "carnet" (passport for personal goods) for my photo equipment. Since I didn't have one—I had never had to show one before—I tried to reason with the officer. In vain. At 11:30 a.m., she sent me back to the customs office in the city of Geneva to get the document. When I arrived there, everyone was on lunch break until 14:00. After providing a deposit of 2,500 Swiss francs, which I had to get in cash from a bank, I finally got the carnet and was able to leave the country after a delay of about five hours.

I experienced my worst disaster with authorities in 2011 at the first Formula 1 Grand Prix in India. A few days before the Grand Prix, I received my visa and did not bother to check it. Although it said Indian Grand Prix as my reason for entry, it also expired on the day of my arrival in New Delhi! At first, the officials wanted to send me back home on the same plane. But then they showed mercy. They sent me from office to office in the Indian capital, but nobody wanted to be responsible for extending my visa. At least this way, I got an unplanned tour of the city. Only after I had filled out what felt like two hundred forms and fought my way through all the official offices for two days, missing the two training days in the process, did I get the necessary stamp. But first I had to pay a fine of one hundred francs for my illegal stay in India.

Stuck in the Elevator

But there were also events that prevented me from taking pictures. There was one in 1998. I was supposed to photograph Williams driver Jacques Villeneuve in Dublin. Shortly before leaving, I stopped to deposit my flash equipment with all the tripods in my photo studio. It was a bitterly cold evening in February. I left my car, a Mercedes 300 TE, with the tailgate open and the radio on in front of the building in the industrial area. Without a jacket, I got into the elevator, hoping to be back a few minutes later. That's when it happened: the elevator stopped between two floors. The building was deserted at night, so I was unable to call for help. Stupidly, no one missed me because I had signed out at home for the trip to Dublin. Only regular exercise saved me from hypothermia. At three o'clock in the morning, the car battery gave up the ghost, and the radio, which had entertained me a little, fell silent. After a sleepless night, I was finally freed around eight in the morning. Of course, there were no pictures from Dublin.

The modern-day shipping of racing cars is much more professional. Whether by truck or aircraft, the cars are placed in a protective "pajama" before loading.

8 "Dani, You Planned This"

A Special Photo Shoot with Michael Schumacher at Monza

Photo shoots are always good for a surprise. I experienced one such surprise during private Ferrari test drives at Monza in July 1997. On the program were special photos with Michael Schumacher for his annual big interview for *Auto, Motor und Sport*. It was envisaged that I would photograph the Ferrari star sitting alone, cross-legged, on the start-finish straight. Then, during the short lunch break, it was time. Michael made his way to the chosen spot, waved to the numerous fans in the stands, and sat down on the hot asphalt. I carefully adjusted my camera. Then it happened. Out of nowhere, someone ran into the picture. As a photographer, I automatically pressed the shutter release, but I didn't know exactly what was really going on. Then I realized that a fan had made his way to the site of the photo shoot despite the barricades. Michael was visibly irritated and his mood worsened. He tried to make it clear to the unknown man that he should leave at once. But that was the last thing on his mind. He calmly took out a small camera and photographed

the then-two-time world champion. And the unbelievable happened, shocking Michael and me—the man approached the Formula 1 star and kissed him on the cheek. Then he disappeared, to great applause from the fans, the same way he had come, over the meter-high security fence in the direction of the grandstand.

The Hype around "Schumi"

Michael was less than thrilled about the unforeseen interruption. Nevertheless, he bore it with composure, and the photo shoot went on as usual. A little later, he returned to the situation and said to me with a laugh, "Dani, I have known you for a long time now. I am sure that you planned the whole thing." And then he added, "There is one thing I would like to ask you for the next time. Could you make sure that the man shaves before he kisses me?"

Of course, I had nothing to do with the kiss. But it resulted in a small, unique picture series that was of great value to me. It was never published, which I find very sad. Only the originally planned, perfectly exposed photo was printed in *Auto, Motor und Sport*. From a purely emotional point of view, however, the three pictures illustrate the unbelievable hype around the person of Michael Schumacher.

The Mud Battle
of My Life

August 15, 1977. After the flood, our small village of Sachseln resembled a huge pile of rubble. Unfortunately, floods and other natural disasters happen again and again, as in Ahrweiler and the surrounding area in 2021.

Normally, mud fights take place on the soaked press parking lots or the sidewalks next to the racetrack. However, I experienced my worst mud battle on August 15, 1997. On that hot and humid summer day, a violent thunderstorm was brewing in the mountains above my hometown of Sachseln. The meteorological situation was unique. Different winds prevented the movement of the cloud masses for a longer time. As a result, all the water in the clouds fell practically on the spot. A storm of the century was created.

In places, up to 1 meter (3.3 feet) of hail fell at higher elevations. In addition, there was endless rain. The mass of water sought its way into the valley and swept away everything that stood in its way. No matter whether trees, sheep, cows, or entire stables: everything was swept toward the valley—until the first bridge. There, everything piled up until the bridge gave way under the enormous pressure. Water and mud now had a free course and flooded the entire village of Sachseln with incredible force.

Sad Mud Bath

At the same time, I was sitting with my then-girlfriend and now-wife, Jeannette, about 10 kilometers (6.2 miles) from Sachseln in a garden restaurant, where it was completely dry. All that we heard and saw was thunder and lightning. Suddenly the waitress told us that it would be best if we went home. All hell had broken loose in Sachseln. She was literally right. We left immediately, but we couldn't go straight home. We had to park the car a good kilometer (0.6 miles) from the village. From there, we made our way on foot. About 100 meters (328 feet) from our home, it was finally over—the quantities of water were much too dangerous. Only hours later, by which time it was already night, did the situation calm down, and we arrived completely soaked at home. What we saw there was a disaster. The basement was knee-deep underwater. A large part of my photo archive had literally drowned in the mud. Another part—negatives, slides, and prints—was floating through the village toward the lake, along with many other things.

A Great Loss

We immediately brought everything that had remained dry to safety. In a second step, we separated the slightly damp things from the wet ones. The next morning, I called Kodak. The company recommended that we immerse the muddy negatives in plastic containers filled with water and deep-freeze the whole thing. Freezing, they said, would stop the chemical reaction. So we took several containers to a cold-storage facility in Lucerne and froze them.

Full of hope, days later we began to thaw and wash the negatives. But soon came the great disillusionment. The high acid content of the mud had attacked the photographic emulsions and thus the actual images too much before freezing. Our immense effort was in vain. My heart bled when I had to throw hundreds of photographic documents into the trash, lost forever.

Frustration within Limits

But there were also positive things: my father never threw anything away. But he was not a proper archivist. So he stored many negatives and slides in hundreds of boxes, which in turn were randomly distributed throughout the archive. Whatever happened to be stored close to the ground had been destroyed by water and mud and had to be thrown away. Since the boxes were stacked randomly, things fell victim across the board and not entire vintages, which again was our good fortune.

By the way, there are certainly pictures "down the drain," which I would have liked to publish in this book. But since I have no idea exactly what is missing, my sense of frustration is not quite as great.

About a third of our archive was destroyed by the mud. Unfortunately, days spent trying to salvage slides and negatives were for naught.

▼▼ A few slides turned into real pieces of art. The mud decomposed the photographic emulsions, and the presence of moisture in the slide envelopes caused the images to shrink. All later attempts to intentionally reproduce this phenomenon failed.

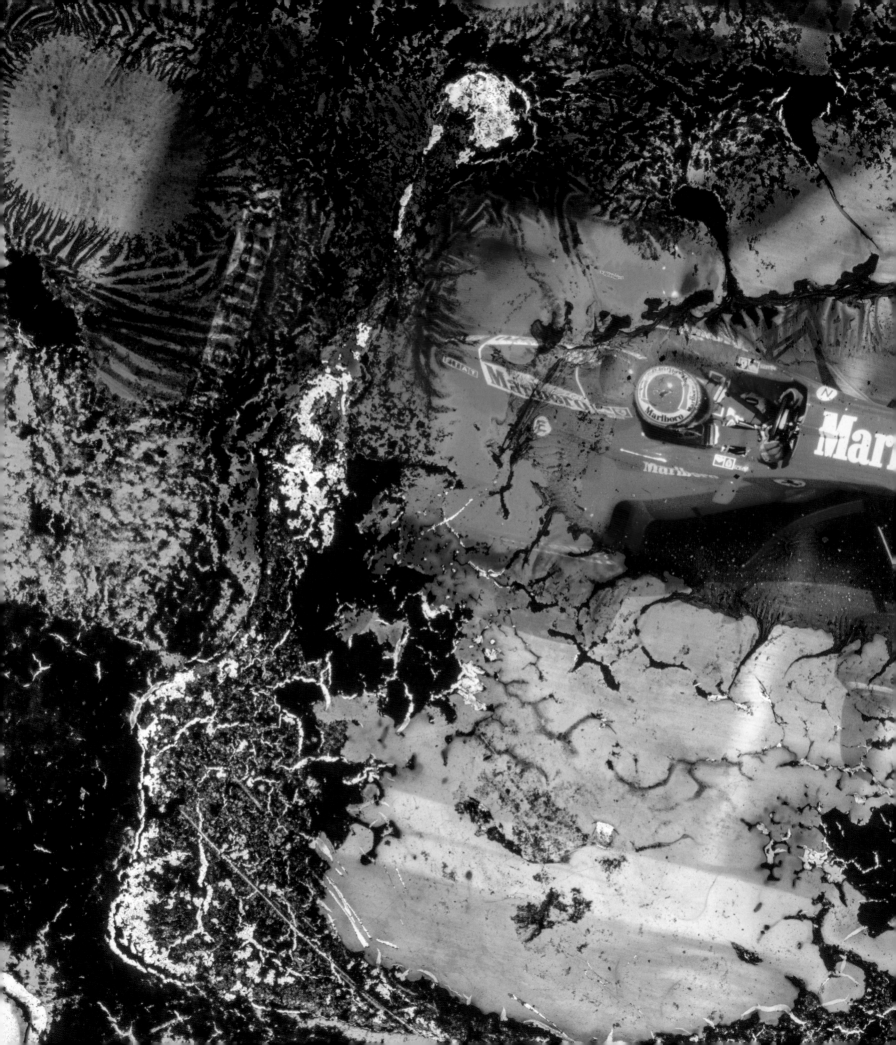

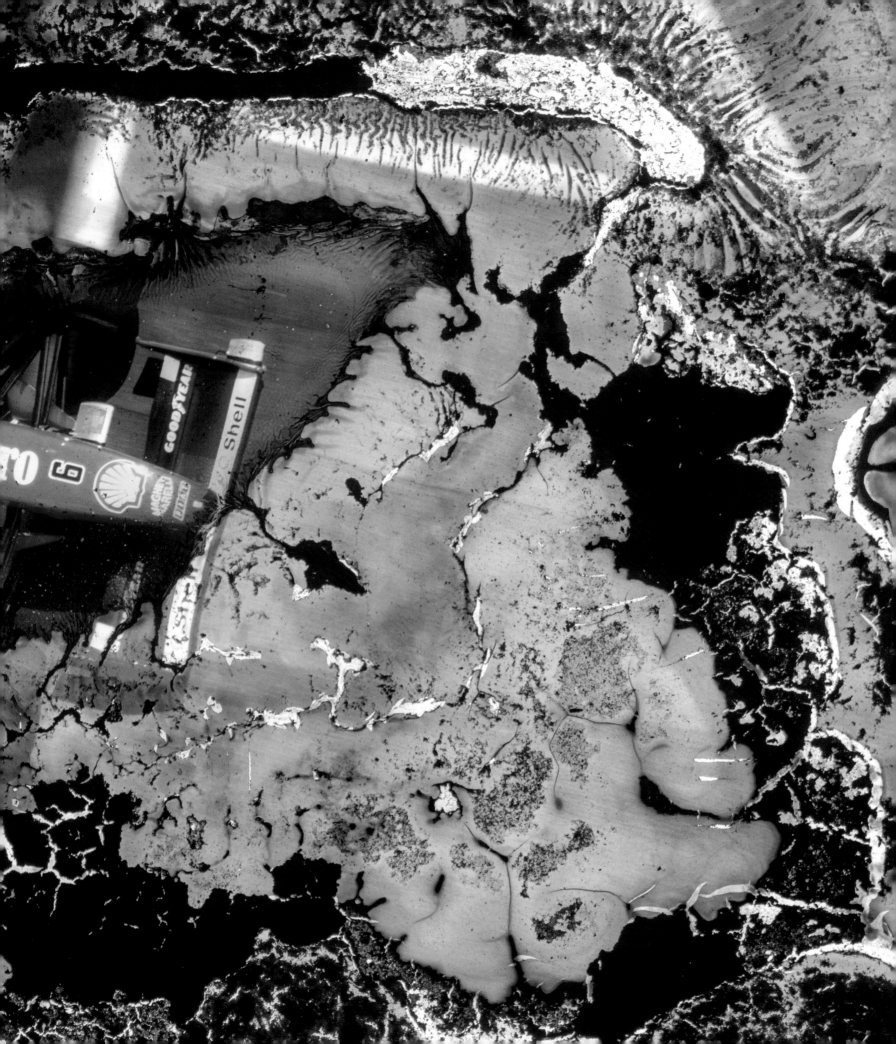

Sparks and Pyrotechnics

Two friends at close quarters. During the night race in Bahrain, Sebastian Vettel (Red Bull) passes Kimi Räikkönen (Ferrari), leaving a shower of sparks.

it's good for the photographers when it's cloudy on the race weekend.

Nowadays, the night races in Singapore, Bahrain, and Abu Dhabi offer optimal conditions for spark-spraying cars. The longer the exposure, the more extensive the streaks caused by the sparks flying away. But it's not quite that easy to capture really great images. The cars can seldom be completely in focus with long exposure times. Due to the impact on the asphalt, the racing car often makes a horizontal movement in addition to the longitudinal one. This then leads to a slight motion blur.

Pyrotechnics

For once, a three-wheeled vehicle provided me with the best story yet featuring brilliant sparks. But it wouldn't have come about without my long-standing friendship with the Swiss sidecar team of Rolf Biland and Kurt Waltisperg. Several times, I was allowed to take pictures for the duo's season preview, including in 1988. To bring even more action into the shots, I suggested a picture with sparking sidecar. Several attempts with titanium plates in various places, even on Kurt Waltisperg's shoes, failed miserably. Then I came up with the idea of pyrotechnics. So I brought ten firework volcanoes in my luggage to Mugello for the first test with the new team. In the meantime, Rolf had attached a corresponding holder to the sidecar.

At the track, I took a seat in the trunk of my Porsche 944 and was chauffeured around the course. Behind me followed the sidecar, which I photographed in the late-evening light. A first test showed that this insane procedure could succeed. Only the first and last seconds of the burning volcano were not suitable for the pictures, because there was too much smoke during this period. We ignited one volcano after the other and continued testing. We had a total of ten tests at our disposal. The difficulty

In 1987, a spectacular phenomenon appeared in Formula 1. The Williams FW11 and the Benetton B187 were the first cars to produce glittering sparks. Photographers and television stations were keen on the new and spectacular images. In the first practice laps at each racetrack, the people behind the cameras had only one question: Where are the sparks flying? But what causes this phenomenon? When the track is uneven, during harsh braking, or if the car is downforced heavily, it hits the racetrack—even more so with full tanks and the corresponding extra weight. At the point of impact, there are titanium blocks that prevent the wooden underbody from being abraded. The contact of the titanium with the asphalt then results in a spectacular shower of sparks. If the daylight is weaker, these are easier to see in the pictures. So was to find the perfect timing of the optimal curve travel with the smokeless phase. In addition, the driving speed could not be too high; otherwise the sparks would be blown away. Since in 1988 I was still shooting slide film, I had no control over the pictures at all. Everything was done by feel. So, in the following days, I waited anxiously for the film to be developed. And lo and behold! The result was exactly as I had wished—an image perfect for me to use for posters and autograph cards.

Biland's biggest competitor, Briton Steve Webster, couldn't believe his eyes when he saw the photo. He immediately contacted Biland and said, "Rolf, what kind of crazy thing have you put on your three wheels again?" In today's digital age, it would be easy to add the sparks through image processing. Back then, however, we as photographers were still really challenged.

▲ A final, sadly less than perfect slide illustrates the pyrotechnics behind Rolf Biland's sidecar. In the analog era, when commissioned work was done, the slides, which were unique, were sold to the customer and were thus lost to us photographers.

▶ DTM (German Touring Car Masters) cars also thrilled the fans with sparks. Here DTM champion Marco Wittmann sprays them at Brands Hatch.

Olivier Grouillard (Fondmetal) at
Jerez in 1991. Heavy clouds filled
the Spanish sky in the early morning
during pre-qualification and provided
perfect conditions for spark photos.

Nigel Mansell in the Williams creates a fireworks display in the Monte Carlo tunnel.

Christmas Card for Nelson Piquet

I took my first good spark picture at the Belgian GP at Spa 1987 as Nelson Piquet in the Williams FW11 took the Eau Rouge Corner. What later became my most famous picture ever was again of the Brazilian, this time in the Benetton B191 (1991). My aspiration to capture a car in the shower of sparks produced by the invisible car in front of it kept me busy for about a year and a half. Again and again, I positioned myself in places where the cars produced sparks, and concentrated on one of the pursuers. For eighteen long months, I was unable to capture the desired image. But then we were in Montreal in 1991. Umpteen films were again sacrificed in the hope of the "winning lottery ticket." Without the slightest idea of what I had photographed, we flew back to Europe on Monday, and soon after I received a call from Michael Schmidt: "Dani, you have taken a sensational picture." It was Nelson Piquet in a shower of sparks from Nigel Mansell. I was doubly lucky, since Nelson had also won the race, after Mansell, who had a huge lead in the last lap, slowed down to wave to the fans and in the process fell victim to an electronics problem just before the finish. Thanks to the victory by the Benetton driver, my picture became the lead story in *Auto, Motor und Sport*. Praise came from all sides, including from Nelson Piquet, who used the picture for his Christmas card. And today a framed enlargement still hangs in his office.

83

9 Vettel, the Ski-Jumper

Attitude Is Everything

What do four-time Olympic ski-jumping champion Simon Ammann and four-time F1 world champion Sebastian Vettel have in common? Their attitude!

The proof: In the parc-fermé at the Malaysian GP on April 4, 2010, winner Sebastian Vettel climbed onto his car as usual and cheered for the team and the photographers. Intuitively, I pressed the shutter release. Only later, when sorting the pictures on my computer, did I realize that the picture actually shows Sebastian Vettel in the position of a ski-jumper just before the jump.

So I put the picture aside in case Swiss ski jumper Simon Ammann should once again attend an F1 Grand Prix. In fact, less than a month later, Sauber informed me that the winter sportsman would be the star guest at the Monaco Grand Prix. With an enlargement of the picture in my luggage, I traveled to the principality. When Simon arrived, I asked him if he would be available for a special promotion. After I had briefly explained to him what it was all about, he agreed. Together we went to see Sebastian at the Red Bull energy station. As agreed, Simon greeted the F1 driver and said he would be very happy to see him get into ski jumping. Seb was completely perplexed and looked at me questioningly. Then Simon pulled the photo out of its sleeve, took a pen, and showed him how he could improve his form. The penny dropped, and they both started laughing. Seb then remarked that this was typical Reinhard again.

Despite all the hustle and bustle and tension, it has always been important to me to also have time for a little fun.

Simon Ammann improves Vettel's stance.

10 The Aliens

John Surtees and Mike Hailwood

I would like to dedicate a chapter to two racers whose achievements I cannot rate highly enough. One is John Surtees. He may well claim a world record for all eternity. Surtees is the only driver in history to have won world championships on two wheels (seven titles) and four wheels (1964 in the Ferrari 158). In addition, he recorded six victories at the TT on the Isle of Man. Later, with the Surtees team, he even fielded his own racing cars in the Formula 1 and the Formula 2 European Championships.

The second legendary racing driver is Mike Hailwood. He was a nine-time motorcycle world champion, fourteen-time Isle of Man TT winner, and Formula 2 European champion (with Surtees!) and also proved his ability with two podium finishes in Formula 1. The Brit drove his only F1 leading laps at the 1971 Italian GP in Monza in a car owned by John Surtees, of all people. He crossed the finish line just 0.18 seconds behind the winner, Peter Gethin. The spectacular thing was that Hailwood finished in only fourth place. Even the fifth-place finisher was only 0.61 seconds short of victory. The race thus went down in Formula 1 history as the one with the closest outcome. It is also described by many as one of the most exciting races ever.

Cars jockeying for the closest finish of all time. In the picture, Chris Amon (Matra) leads François Cevert (Tyrrell), Mike Hailwood (Surtees), Ronnie Peterson (March), and the eventual winner, Peter Gethin (BRM). Jackie Stewart said of the slipstream battles at Monza: "If you go into the last lap in first place, you've lost the race."

◀ Mike Hailwood on the MV Agusta at the 1964 Solitude GP, where he won the 500cc class—four years after John Surtees's success (1960). He also became world champion that year.

Surtees and His Six Most Important Wheels

John Surtees maintained a great friendship with my father for many years. He even visited him once in Switzerland. Many years later, I also developed a very good relationship with him. At the Ennstal Classic in 2002, I had the privilege of sitting beside him in the Mercedes 300 SL prototype of 1952, an honor that my father had experienced in 1964 at Reims in the Ferrari 250 LM.

In 2014, I was part of an unforgettable photo shoot at Surtees's wonderful estate in the county of Kent. He had invited me and motorsport editor Michael Schmidt to go there. The reason was a very special one. For once, Surtees's garage contained not only his 500 cc MV Agusta, with which he had won the motorcycle world championship title four times, but also the Ferrari 158 in which he had won the Formula 1 World Championship in 1964. The race car had come to England from the USA for the Goodwood Revival and was temporarily stored at Surtees's for a few days.

I was the last photographer who was allowed to photograph him with his two most successful vehicles before his death in 2017. After the shoot, the good-humored John took the time to make us coffee and tea in his kitchen.

"So Fucking Unique"

In 2018, I fulfilled a long-awaited dream, one that unfortunately was never feasible in F1 times, and visited the TT on the Isle of Man. The TT—as it is usually just called—is considered the oldest and most dangerous motorcycle race in the world. Having seen and in particular photographed just about everything in car racing on this globe, at this race I felt like I was in the twilight zone. I believe that this event can be compared only to the legendary Hahnenkamm ski race on the Streif in Kitzbühel, the Targa Florio road races in Sicily, the Mille Miglia in northern Italy, or the F1 races through the green hell of the Nürburgring. The speed of these motorcycles on completely normal country roads without any camber is so outrageous that you just have to take your hat off to all the drivers. Two-time DTM champion Marco Wittmann commented, "Compared to them, we're just schoolboys." Horst Saiger of Austria, a competitor in a number of TT races, summed it up as follows: "For those who have raced here once, everything else, including every other race, is just child's play." And living motorcycle legend Valentino Rossi said, "I rode one lap on the Isle of Man, and I immediately realized why people love it so much; because it's so fucking unique. It's incredible, fantastic, but unfortunately also way too dangerous."

▲▲ Mike Hailwood

▲ John Surtees

▶ Monza 1971. Team manager John Surtees talking to his driver Mike Hailwood

▶▶ John Surtees with girlfriend while visiting us in Sachseln in 1964

John Surtees sitting on the MV Agusta at the ripe old age of eighty, with the Ferrari 158 in the background. He became world champion with both vehicles.

In 2018, Peter Hickmann won the legendary Senior TT on the isle of Man.

11 Silent Concert

The Formula E: Don't Touch!

The technical revolution is automatically creating its own new Formula 1, featuring electric cars, called Formula E. Completely silent, the cars are winding their way through the world's inner cities and delivering exciting races.

Since the era of hoarsely rattling hybrid turbo engines, Formula 1 has lost much of its appeal. In the era of high-revving and deafening V10 engines, if you asked a visitor attending a Grand Prix for the first time what impressed him most, the answer was always the same: the engine noise! In every corner of the Principality of Monaco, one could follow the race cars around the entire track, solely by the sound in one's ears. And now, suddenly car races are taking place, and people sitting in the sunny garden restaurant just a few meters from the track hear absolutely nothing. Completely crazy!

Electrocution

Formula E presents the photographer with completely different working conditions compared to Formula 1. To work as a photographer and receive the necessary photo vest, a briefing must be completed. It's made clear that the cars must not be touched in any way. There's a risk of electrocution! At the same time, it's pointed out to the participants that the racing cars do not make any noise. One must be careful not to be run over. It's quite different in the pit lane of a screaming Formula 1 race, where you can always hear much more than you actually see, and you can also feel the powerful air vibrations in the abdominal region, so that not even a deaf person need fear being hit by a car.

Whirring Sewing Machines

In Formula E, the pit lane has been declared a danger zone. Music headphones, which distract from what is happening on the track, are forbidden. In Formula 1, the idea of photographing with sound in one's ear would never have been considered. Even the loudest rock music would have been drowned out by the roar of the engines. In Formula 1, ears must be protected at all costs to avoid hearing loss. Once I was kneeling behind a 2-liter sports car when the engine started without warning, and the inner workings of my right ear were almost blown out of my head.

When it comes to action shots on the track, there's another problem. Just like in ski races, one can hardly hear the subjects approaching. One must maintain full concentration behind the camera and always be ready, in order to avoid missing the sudden appearance of the racing cars, which whiz past whirring like sewing machines.

When BMW entered the FE market in 2018 with the iFE.18, I was able to photograph the car in a Munich studio.

Whenever the car's underbody touches the curb, one hears a sound reminiscent of a crash. Without the engine noise, one suddenly also hears the squealing of the tires.

Alexander Sims slows down in the Moroccan backlight.

Thanks to the absence of noise pollution and CO_2 emissions, Formula E has the great advantage of being able to drive in city centers. The picture shows the pit lane in Paris on the Esplanade des Invalides.

In the event of an accident, such as this one involving Jaime Alguersuari (Virgin) in Monaco in 2015, "Please don't touch" naturally also applies to the track marshals.

Not all that glitters is gold. The huge interest in Formula E initially shown by the factories is already crumbling again. André Lotterer in the DS Techeetah FE in Morocco 2018.

The Family Camera History

Fortunately, I have sold hardly any of our cameras. The result is another exciting story. Here are the two cameras my father used in the 1950s—the Leica lllc 35mm and the Rolleiflex 6 x 6 medium format.

his first camera, the 1600F, to the world in New York on October 6, 1948. It was designed by industrial designer Sixten Sason, who also worked for Saab. An absolutely ingenious feature was its modular system, which allowed the exchange not only of lenses, but also of viewfinders and film magazines. Since the camera struggled with major teething problems as a result of its fastest shutter speed of 1/1600, the 1000F soon followed. It was somewhat slower at 1/1000 and was on the market from 1952 to 1957. To go with it, Dallmeyer released the 508 mm f5.6 telephoto lens, of course still without a diaphragm and with somewhat limited format illumination. As a result, the corners of the image remained black. To exaggerate slightly, the result was a round image on the negative. Despite this limitation, this camera-lens combination was made for motorsports, and my father shot about 70 percent of his pictures with it.

There were two types of film for use in professional medium-format cameras: Type 120 roll film with twelve exposures in 6 × 6 cm (2.36 × 2.36 inch) format and Type 220 with twenty-four exposures. The later 6 × 7 cm (2.36 x 2.75 inch) Asahi Pentax medium-format camera, which looked like a blown-up 35 mm SLR, took ten exposures on a 120 and twenty-one on a 220 film. At that time, there was no possibility of fast series of images. One needed a great deal of experience to get a perfect picture. First, the focus had to be set, then the correct aperture had to be selected. The photographer had to remember that the viewfinder image became dark due to the lack of a spring aperture. Then, after shooting, the film had to be advanced manually. So it was possible to take only one picture of the start of a race.

It was particularly difficult to capture vehicles that appeared out of nowhere. One had to focus by feel, aim quickly, and then press the shutter release at the all-important moment. Today, of course, such "golden" moments are much easier to capture with the help of autofocus and digital technology.

Julius Weitmann, probably the best-known motorsports photographer of the 1950s, photographed mainly with a Graflex Super D. The great advantage of this bulky-looking camera was its ability to use large-format sheet film as well as modern film packs, roll film, and even 35mm negative strips. With the fastest shutter speed of one-thousandth of a second, it was predestined for dynamic sports photography. Weitmann appreciated the robust camera because of its fast shutter speeds and outstanding image sharpness.

My father started motorsport photography in 1950. At that time, the Graflex Super D had already passed its zenith, and new and better cameras were available. So in the beginning my father shot his photographs with a Rolleiflex 6 × 6 cm medium-format camera and a Leica IIIc 35mm that he shared with his father. Then, in 1957, he switched to the Hasselblad.

The Medium Format

Swedith photographer Victor Hasselblad unveiled

The Pentax 6 × 7 arrived on the market in 1969. After the Hasselblad, it became the standard for high-quality action photography. The body with the interchangeable viewfinder prisms had a double bayonet lens mount, consisting of an inner mount for lenses up to 300 mm and an outer mount for all longer focal lengths. The inner port offered the helpful jumping aperture, while the outer one still had the darkening in the viewfinder by stopping down. The fixed 400 mm lens offered sensational image quality and just about worked without a tripod. The extremely heavy 600 mm lens, on the other hand, could be operated only with a tripod. Nevertheless, some of our shots were taken with it. Less optimal was the large, heavy mirror, which led to slight camera shake every now and then when shooting with somewhat longer exposure times.

The Hasselblad with the Dallmeyer telephoto lens and the Nikon F came into use in the 1960s. Hasselblad's great advantage was its interchangeable magazines, so that photographs could be taken in both black and white and color with little effort. Later came the Pentax 6 x 7 in medium format and the Nikon F2 in 35mm.

This black-and-white negative is from the Hasselblad with the Dallmeyer telephoto lens and clearly shows the somewhat rounded image, since the corners of the 6 x 6 cm negative were not exposed.

Here is a size comparison of a 24 x 36 mm (0.94 x 1.4 in.), a 6 x 6 cm (2.36 x 2.36 in.), and a 6 x 7 cm (2.36 x 2.75 in.) slide. The larger the slide, the more image information is available, which leads to better-quality cropped images and allows much larger paper enlargements.

I used the Pentax 6 × 7 for the first time on April 13, 1980, at the Formula 2 race in Hockenheim, where the Austrian Markus Höttinger had a fatal accident. After that, we used this very good medium-format camera for years at our motorsport events, like our professional colleagues Ulrich Schwab and Hans Peter Seufert.

The 35 mm Format

The archetype of today's 35 mm SLR camera was launched by Nikon in 1959 as the "F" model. With its 1:1 viewfinder image, and a modular system of viewfinder and lenses, it soon became the world's best working tool for professional sports, reportage, fashion, and science photography. My father bought one in the early 1960s as a replacement for the Leica and was delighted with it. It was only after fourteen years, in October 1973, that it was replaced by the F2. I acquired this model in 1976, when I started photographing the Swiss championship.

It was my faithful companion for years. In the 1980s, I switched to the F3. By the way, Canon was nowhere near as innovative back then as it is today. It wasn't until March 1970 that it launched a camera that could catch up with Nikon, the F1 model.

In 1994, I switched from the Nikon FM2 to Canon because Canon had developed a much better autofocus system. The mechanism was in the optics and not in the camera body like the competition. I first used the EOS1N on May 1 at Imola, the day Ayrton Senna was killed in an accident. I used various other EOS models until I switched to my first digital camera.

Telephoto Lenses

For a long time, the technology of long focal lengths could not keep up with the level of the cameras—at least as far as sports photography was concerned. Nevertheless, a first milestone was the Nikkor-Reflex 500mm f8 mirror telephoto lens, which was launched in 1968. This very short but thick telephoto lens featured a fixed aperture of f8. Exposure had to be adjusted based on the basis of shutter speed or ISO values (analogous to ASA film sensitivities). All bright points out of focus got the "donut effect" characteristic of this optic. The lens thus produced a very special and unique image blur. With the light and relatively small lens, very special shots were possible in good lighting conditions.

In 1969, the Zoom Nikkor 80–200 mm f 4.5 AI was released. It was a lens that was perfect for action photography and is still one of the most important lenses today. Meanwhile, it offers a lens speed of f 2.8 and is equipped with a rotating ring for focal length adjustment. The first variants were still sliding zooms. One changed the focal length by sliding the wide focusing ring back and forth. Probably by accident, the zoom effect images were created. In these, the focal length is changed during the exposure. The result is a speed effect that sweeps from the inside to the outside. The sharpness is retained in the center of the image, while the wiping effect increases more and more toward the edge of the image. Race cars are particularly well suited to this technique, but it is difficult to control and produces a lot of waste. With today's rotating zooms, it has become more difficult to achieve a reasonable zoom effect without a tripod.

Digital Cameras

Canon had been in the digital market together with Kodak since 1997. In 2000, Canon introduced the first in-house digital EOS. This camera, with a Kodak digital back, was sinfully expensive. It cost around 50,000 DM ($22,500), and the image quality was much worse than a cell phone shot today. The big push came after the millennium, when suddenly digital cameras of immense quality conquered the market. In 2000, Canon introduced its first in-house digital EOS. I myself entered digital photography in 2002 with a Canon D30. Those who continued to work in analog were left with no chance against their competitors. If you compare excellent Kodachrome slides with modern digital images, there are worlds between them. In addition to the possibility of subsequent brightness and contrast control, as well as color control, the immense sensitivity of the sensors suddenly made it possible to take pictures of excellent quality under miserable lighting conditions and without the aid of atmosphere-destroying flash units. The main advantage was not only their better image quality, but also their ultrafast processing and easier transmission of images. After the D30, I used various other models, including the EOS1 D, EOS1 D Mark ll, EOS1 D Mark lll, and EOS1 DX.

My current standard equipment for a race weekend includes, like most of my colleagues, three camera bodies (Canon EOS 1D X Mark ll and soon the Mark lll), plus two zoom lenses: 24–70mm and 70–200mm, as well as two telephoto lenses with fixed focal lengths of 400 and 600 mm. In addition, I also use a 1.4 teleconverter to extend the telephoto focal lengths of the two lenses a little more if possible.

The screen of digital cameras replaces the Polaroid of the analog professional photographer. With it, one can easily and quickly control everything and have 100% certainty about the desired image.

12 The Space Shuttle

Jewel of a Racing Car

Racing cars are aesthetic. They attract people with their shape and color. There are extremely attractive cars and also really ugly ones. But the special thing is that successful racing cars are often called beautiful. This is despite the fact that the designers do not focus on aesthetics. Tony Southgate of Arrows commented, "Your only job is to be fast. If your car has the pole position, people will envy you even if it's ugly." I'm not a big tech geek. I'm more interested in the people who make motorsports come alive. Nevertheless, there are a few cars in particular that fascinate me.

Auto Union

Of the racing cars of the prewar era, I am particularly enthusiastic about the Auto Union Type C with the V-16 mid-engine from 1936–37. It's not just the look of this model that strikes me. The sound of the mighty 16-cylinder engine is also so impressive that it makes one forget everything else. I had the opportunity to photograph the replica with Hans Joachim Stuck at the 2017 Großglockner Grand Prix. It was an emotional experience for me to photograph this incredibly beautiful car, with its 6 liters (366 cubic inches) of displacement, sixteen cylinders, Roots blower (compressor), and 520 horsepower, with a weight of just 750 kilograms (1,653 lbs.), against the insane backdrop of the freshly snow-covered Großglockner. I can think of only superlatives for this car.

An Alfetta on the apron of the Bern-Belp airport

◀ The Gotthard carriage with two thoroughbred horses from Maranello on the historic Gotthard Road, the Tremola

The Sauber C21 (2002) with an unusual backdrop

The BMW Sauber F1.06 in the Ciudad de las Artes y las Ciencias (City of Arts and Sciences) in Valencia, an architectural design by Santiago Calatrava. Before the presentation of the vehicle, early in the morning at six o'clock, I managed to convince the people responsible to let me take this picture, which then had to be in the can in just under fifteen minutes.

Tyrrell Project 34

The second design that strikes me as inspired was at the starting line of the F1 world championship in 1976. It was the Tyrrell Project 34 with its six wheels. When I first saw the car in *Motorsport Aktuell*, I thought it was an April Fool's joke. Ken Tyrrell had promised his driver Jody Scheckter a revolution for the new season. But when he saw the six-wheeled car for the first time, he was extremely skeptical. Today, he finds the six-wheeled Tyrrell much better than when he was active. According to Scheckter, he had always underestimated the car and was sure that only its strict dependence on tire manufacturer Goodyear had prevented even better results. The South African thus addressed the Achilles' heel of the car. Goodyear had to produce the special small tires for the Tyrrell and neglected further development over time. This is also illustrated by the results. In 1976 the P34 achieved a double victory at the Swedish GP and several other good results. The following year, it was less and less competitive, and at the end of the season, Tyrrell had to bury the concept of the six-wheeled Formula 1 car.

Incidentally, the P 34 came from the pen of Derek Gardner. The car reflected the spirit of the times. In the 1970s, a great deal was still planned and built on the basis of pure instinct and the inner obsession of a single designer. For this reason, there were various curious and wayward cars on the starting grid. Gardner described the time: "Of course, the lack of knowledge is what makes this profession so exciting. If racing were really grasped and understood, it would cease to be an art. It would become a science and perhaps appeal to many more people. But it would run the risk of losing its magic." His words have certainly proven true in recent years as Formula 1 has become more and more of a science.

Sure, there are other race cars I bow down to: the Lancia-Ferrari D50 (1956), the Ferrari P4 (1967), the Chaparral 2D (1966) and 2F (1967), the Porsche 917 LH (1971), the Ferrari 312T (1975), the Lotus 79 (1978), and the McLaren-Porsche MP4 2 (1984). The last really nice car was the Jordan 191 (1991). Michael Schumacher began his great career with it.

Failed Calendar Idea

I have always had a fascination for photographing racing cars in unusual surroundings. Unfortunately, it's very difficult and usually extremely costly to transport a car from A to B for a shot. For Credit Suisse, the Sauber sponsor at the time, I once came up with the idea for a special picture calendar titled *Made in Switzerland*. I wanted to photograph the current car at twelve typical Swiss tourist locations such as the Matterhorn, Lake Lucerne, the Rhine Falls, or the Eiger Monch and Jungfrau. Unfortunately, the idea came to naught due to funding issues. Nevertheless, there were always opportunities to take special pictures; for example, in Kuala Lumpur. For Sauber and later BMW Sauber, an annual photo shoot with the Malaysian sponsor Petronas was scheduled in front of the Twin Towers of the same name. But the small, flat car could never be meaningfully reconciled with the mighty towers. When I described my problem to the Petronas marketing person in charge, she asked me what needed to be done differently. I spontaneously said that the car should be positioned in such a way that it would look like a space shuttle lifting off from its launchpad. When I returned to Kuala Lumpur the next year, I was amazed. In front of me, the Formula 1

The McLaren M8 CanAm race car, photographed at the McLaren Technology Center in Woking. The architecture was designed by Norman Foster.

car was actually standing in a vertical position on a moving ramp. The result was a unique picture, and this extraordinary effort was rewarded. No other photograph of a BWM Sauber F1 has been printed more often.

The Auto Union Type C on the Großglockner

Ready for launch! The BMW Sauber 1 space shuttle in Kuala Lampur. This somewhat special picture was the result of a spontaneous, crazy idea and a little effort.

Jo Siffert's March 701 (1970) posing in
an unusual location—a parking garage!

The Ferrari F2007 was photographed in front of the windows of Enzo's former office in Fiorano.

13 The Picture That Ron Dennis Couldn't Buy

The 1998 GP USA in Detroit

As a photographer, I am always seeking fresh perspectives. Sometimes, I begin thinking about where and how I might be able to take a very special picture days before a GP weekend.

Often, however, outstanding photographs were the result of a spontaneous idea—in 1998, for example, during training for the US Grand Prix in Detroit.

There was a house with fans on the roof right next to the street circuit. I wondered if there would be an exciting perspective from up there. I then approached the security guards at the entrance to the house, and they finally allowed me to use the roof terrace for a quarter of an hour. Once up there, I was disappointed. The view was in no way any better. On the contrary: the trees hung far over the racetrack, and the cars rushed past under the green leaves. To avoid embarrassment, I waited out the fifteen minutes and disappointedly photographed through the trees

with a slower shutter speed. I left the roof at the appointed time and went on photographing at the track. The surprise came days later. Of all things, my roof shot became the lead story with the title "There's Something in the Bushes," and everyone, including the picture editor and layout artist of Sport Auto, was enthusiastic about the picture.

Not for Sale

At the annual big Hugo Boss party during the German Grand Prix in Heidelberg, the photo was awarded a special prize. The next day, I was summoned to the office of Ron Dennis. He wanted to buy the "bush picture" from me. But to his surprise, I refused to accept his offer. Incidentally, this was the only time in my forty-year career as a motorsport photographer that I refused to sell a picture. The reason: although he had worked his way up from a simple mechanic to a McLaren boss and had a flawless career, Ron was unrivaled in his arrogance. Once he even publicly referred to us photographers as "annoying vermin." How low would I have had to sink to sell a picture to someone like that?

Ayrton Senna (McLaren-Honda MP4/4), Detroit 1998

111

14 Bad Luck Squared

From Racing Car to Handcycle

Alessandro "Alex" Zanardi is a racing icon with a history that is not really enviable but extremely moving. His appearances in the premier class were not crowned with success. In forty-one races, he scored just one world championship point in five different cars—in 1993, he finished sixth at the Brazilian Grand Prix in a Lotus-Ford.

The Accident

Zanardi became world famous only much later, due to a brutal and dramatic accident in the 2001 Champ Car race at the Lausitzring. The two-time CART champion (1997 and 1998) had to be resuscitated seven times after the crash on September 15 and lost both his legs. But he fought his way back into life and motorsport. Time and again, he surprised interviewers and the audience with pointed statements.

"For me, it wasn't a bad time," he said. "I was asleep, after all. And when I woke up, I was happy to be alive. German doctors gave me so much blood that they should issue me a German passport," he said. "Everyone asked if I would get back in the car. But my first goal was to be able to pee by myself."

In 2011, Alex Zanardi launched his second, much greater career in the handcycle discipline, winning six medals at the Paralympic Games, four of them gold. He never lost even a hint of zest for life. "My accident became the great opportunity of my life," he said several times.

On the Road to Triumph

The Italian passed his toughest athletic test in 2014. He won the Ironman in Hawaii, the toughest triathlon in the world, in the category of physically challenged athletes. In the process, he completed the race with a 3.6-kilometer (2.2 mile) swim, 180 kilometers (112 miles) of handcycling, and the final marathon in a wheelchair under the magic ten-hour mark. He repeated the triumph again the following year. His motto was "Behind every great champion, you'll find the word 'passion,' and not so much ambition."

Williams driver and later shooting star Alex Zanardi at the Japanese Grand Prix at Suzuka (1999)

Finishing the Race

Two years after his accident at the Lausitzring, Alex finally finished the race. In the Reynard Indy Car, which was specially modified for him, he showed his great class even without legs. With his prostheses and two canes, he hobbled to the car and sat in the cockpit. I was allowed to accompany him with my camera every step of the way. Always inhibited by his disability, I nevertheless pressed the shutter release at the decisive moments. It was incredibly impressive how he mastered it all after only two years. All alone on the huge trioval, he then completed the thirteen laps that he had lacked to win in 2001. His lap times were at an absolute top level. He would even have qualified for the race as fifth fastest!

In 2018, Zanardi was a guest starter at the German Touring Car Masters night race at Misano. He drove a BMW M4 DTM to an incredible fifth place in the second race. At the finish, he was celebrated like a world champion, and the press conference had to be cut short at some point due to time constraints.

Photos were always important to Alex Zanardi. Two that are associated with special emotions hang in his living room. "One is from my first win after my accident in the WTCC at Oschersleben in 2005. It shows the moment when I'm leaning on the podium fence above a huge crowd of fans as well as the whole WTCC [World Touring Car Championship] community and being showered with champagne by Jörg Müller and Andy Priaulx. It always brings out in me all the emotions associated with that particular achievement. The second is emotionally very similar and was taken at Brands Hatch in 2012, right after the handcycle time trial where I won the gold medal [at the Paralympics]. This unique snapshot, in which I'm holding my handcycle in the air like a trophy right after the finish line, captures all the excitement, satisfaction, and joy, and all the pride that I felt in that moment."

And Fight Again

Unfortunately, bad luck remained with Alex Zanardi. On June 19, 2020, he crashed his handcycle in the Objettivo Tricolore race. He ran into the oncoming lane, collided with a truck, and suffered serious head injuries. Since then, the likable Italian has been fighting his way back to life one more time.

> All alone on the huge trioval, he then completed the thirteen laps that he had lacked to win in 2001. His lap times were at the absolute top level.

What an incredible will to live this person has. In 2003, he drove the final thirteen laps of his missed victory at the Lausitzring (2001) with prosthetic legs.

Zanardi's fifth-place finish in the
DTM night race at Misano in 2018 was
celebrated like a victory by us all.

After Zanardi's serious handcycle accident (2020), even Pope Francis reached out to him. Since then, he has been fighting to get his life back for the second time. Keep fighting, Alex!

15 . . . And If the Tire Bursts

The Black Gold

The 1,000 km Monza 1969. The Firestone tires on the 312P could not withstand the pressure of the car. The tread came off, and Peter Schetty spun out in training while braking in the Parabolica. Pieces of the tire flew off and ruined the rear suspension. Enzo Ferrari contacted the tire manufacturer and received confirmation of a production error—air bubbles had become lodged between the casing and the tread.

Pedro Rodriguez started the race from the second row and, while in the lead, handed the Ferrari over to Peter Schetty. Shortly afterward, there was another puncture. After the necessary repair and the resulting loss of time, the Mexican got back into the cockpit. He didn't get far, however, and after sixty-six laps a third puncture ended his race.

New Zealander Chris Amon was gripped by pure fear before the start, and so he stopped the sister car after only 39 laps with a deliberately over-revving engine.

The purpose of the tires is simple. They transfer the drive and braking forces of the race car to the track surface. Since thousandths of a second are at stake in motorsport, they perform an important function. If a racing team catches the optimum temperature window of the rubber surface through the right setting, the tire transfers the engine power perfectly to the ground. The result: the tire clings to the asphalt like a gecko. When braking, it restrains the forward momentum, guides the car through the

curve as if on rails, and transfers all the engine power to the asphalt during the subsequent acceleration. Taking all this into account, it's not surprising that tires often lead to endless discussions among teams and drivers. One often gets the feeling that victory and defeat depend solely on them.

Even the narrow tires of the 1950s were decisive. Pirelli was the most successful, followed by Firestone and Dunlop. In the 1980s, so-called qualifying tires

◄ Christian Fittipaldi (Minardi) rattles to the finish on two wheels after a backflip at the 1993 Italian GP.

If the rubber fails to withstand the pressure . . .

Derek Warwick in the Brabham has his left rear tire burst at 300 kph (186 mph) on the start-finish straight at Zeltweg (1986).

came into use—special soft tires made for just one lap. Black gold (rubber) is also associated with triumph and defeat. In 1986, Nigel Mansell lost the world championship to Alain Prost at the Australian GP because his left rear tire exploded shortly before the end of the race.

Winning the Lottery

A photographer always faces the pressure of being in the right place at the right time. The year 1986 was such a moment. I was on the start-finish straight at Zeltweg, just a few hundred meters before the braking point of what was then the Hella-Licht (Hella Lighting) chicane. Then, unexpectedly, the left rear tire of Derek Warwick's Brabham burst. My Nikon, which was equipped with a motor drive, unintentionally took a second shot. The

car had already moved out of focus, but despite the blur, one can clearly see the tire coming off the rim. Warwick then lost control of the Brabham and was catapulted into the air by the guardrail. I had the presence of mind to capture this moment as well. With today's autofocus system, both pictures would probably have been crisp. Catching such a moment is comparable to picking all six winning numbers in the lottery.

Racing cars with tire remnants on the rim are rewarding photo subjects. In the meantime, there are many large screens at the race track so that the spectators in the stands can follow all the racing action. The screens also help us photographers. In this way, we find out early on if a driver has experienced a puncture and can prepare for the arrival of the damaged car at the side of the track.

In photographic terms, this picture of Wilson Fittipaldi, Emerson's brother, hitting the wall in the swimming pool chicane at Monte Carlo in 1975 in the Copersucar and tearing off his right front wheel, must be seen as a pure stroke of luck.

Bernhard Bauer in the Tecno 68 Bernhard
Baur pulls out of the F3 preliminary race in
Monaco in 1969.

Unlike in an F1 car, which reacts highly sensitively to any impact, a puncture feels different in a rally car. I experienced this in Catalonia during test drives in a Ford Focus as Armin Schwarz's co-driver. Suddenly the latter said, "Oh sh**," to me. I was surprised and asked him what was going on. Schwarz replied, "We have a puncture in the right rear." Unlike the driver, I hadn't noticed the damage on the bumpy gravel road, nor did I have the feeling that I was traveling slower. Only at the service point did the proof come when I saw the battered fender and the rubberless rim.

The Biggest Disappointment

But how is a racing tire actually made? That's exactly what we wanted to capture for *Auto, Motor und Sport* in 2003 and asked Michelin in Clermont-Ferrand if we could photograph the production of a racing tire. The answer was a resounding "yes," but with the condition that the pictures had to be digital so that the factory could check them. No sooner said than done! We traveled to the Massif Central, and I spent the whole day taking photographs in the dark factory hall with a lot of illumination. After the work was done, I handed over the memory cards to the person responsible for the media. A short time later, at the end of the coffee break, I received them back. What followed was the biggest disappointment of my photographic career. With the exception of a few

What followed was the biggest disappointment of my photographic career. I drove home completely frustrated.

insignificant pictures, Michelin had pulled all the data from the card and destroyed it or transferred it to its own archive. I had clearly adhered to all the agreements we had made, and had not photographed anything that had not been approved on-site. Completely frustrated, we traveled home.

One of the safety measures introduced after Ayrton Senna's fatal accident was the installation of wheel tethers connecting the wheels to the chassis to prevent the wheels from coming free during an accident.

125

Johnny Herbert passes the strug-
gling but still leading Williams driven
by Ralf Schumacher at the Nürburgring (1999) and wins the first and only
Grand Prix for Jackie Stewart's team.

Alex Caffi in the Dallara had to limp back to the pits after blowing a tire on the 6.8-km (4.2-mile) Hockenheimring in 1988. The picture shows him in the east corner.

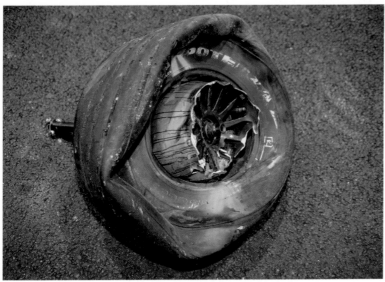

▲▲+▲▲▶ Kamui Kobayashi plows through the gravel bed of the first corner after a start crash at the Australian Grand Prix (2014).

▲ Relic of a crime. In Singapore (2008), Flavio Briatore ordered Nelsinho Piquet to deliberately put the Renault into the wall in order to help his teammate Fernando Alonso win the 800th GP with the aid of the safety car rules.

▲▶ The ugly, grooved slicks (1998–2008) were meant to reduce the increasing cornering speeds.

▶ Did that cost me the world championship? A pensive Jody Scheckter (Wolf WR1) after his retirement at the 1977 French GP in Dijon.

▲ Knocked-off wheels often became dangerous projectiles and had to be retrieved.

▲▶ When racing was still a great platform for *Playboy* and *Penthouse*

▶ Monzanapolis (1957–58), the race of the two worlds, where the Formula 1 cars competed against the American Champ Cars. Pat O`Connor drove 226 miles on the Monza oval during the test for Firestone, with an average speed of more than 273 kph [169.6 mph] (at Indianapolis his average for pole position was 231.7 kph [144 mph]).

▲▲+▲▲▶ A look inside the F1 wheel rim production facility for Ferrari at BBS (*above*)

▲+▲▶ Two of the very few remaining pictures of Michelin's tire production facility in Clermont-Ferrand

The optimum temperature window for racing tires is 80 to 100 degrees Celsius (176 to 212 degrees Fahrenheit). Weaving motions keep the tires at the right temperature during the opening lap or behind the safety car. At low air temperatures, one can clearly see the heat rising from tires that have just been removed.

A snapshot from the second chicane, the Variante della Roggia at Monza (1996), where Michael Schumacher (Ferrari) and Jacques Villeneuve (Williams) were surprised by errant tires.

Walter Brun with total commitment for the photographer. At that time, it was still possible to drive and take photographs on a public road without any protection. Today, both parties involved would certainly end up in prison.

only was a photographer but also ran his own postcard publishing company, he acquired companies such as Firestone and Valvoline as customers. They had tens of thousands of autograph cards printed by him, such as those of Graham Hill and Jim Clark. At the same time, many racing drivers continued to order cards directly from Josef. These included Jo Siffert and Walter Brun.

At the Dutch Grand Prix at Zandvoort in 1968, there was a shoot for tire manufacturer Firestone. The company had clear ideas about how the drivers had to be placed with the cars. Unfortunately, my father's English was less than perfect, and since there were also drivers on the list whom my father did not know personally, he asked Jo Siffert for help. He immediately stepped in as an assistant and ordered his fellow racers to the desired position. My father photographed driver after driver. Nowadays, something like that is unthinkable.

A Unique Shoot

An unbelievable story from today's point of view happened in 1963, when Walter Brun from central Switzerland started his first racing season in a Lotus Cortina. As a young and ambitious driver, he naturally needed autograph cards. And these had to be available for his first race. Without further ado, a photo shoot was organized, but not on a racetrack. No, no!

Walter Brun and my father, Josef, chose a curve on the public mountain road from Giswil to Sörenberg and turned it into their racetrack. To make the pictures look professional, Walter drove the Lotus Cortina through the curve five or six times at high speed on a very cold but dry spring day. That's how his first autograph card came into being—just in time for his first race.

The oldest autograph card comes from the Bavarian King Ludwig ll. He began signing photos of himself after his accession to the throne in 1864 and gave the pictures away. Over time, autograph cards became increasingly popular, and collectors organized themselves into swap meets. In 1968, a working group of autograph collectors developed in Germany.

In the early days of motorsports, drivers ordered and managed their cards themselves. It was not until the late 1960s, especially with the increased presence of sponsors, that the subjects were created according to the wishes of the financiers. To get the best possible exposure for their logos, the sponsors began to commission their own photo shoots. Since my father not

Fully Organized

When I started taking pictures in 1976, there were only a few racers who still ordered autograph cards directly from us. One exception was Gregor Foitek. Internationally, the orders now came through the teams, the factories, the management, or the sponsors.

In F1, professionalization increased sharply in the 1990s. So-called film and photo days came into being. These usually took place after the vehicle presentation at the subsequent first function test.

From 2006 to 2009, I photographed for BMW Sauber and was on assignment for BMW Motorsport in Munich. Shortly before the start of each season, there were two special photo days, and two other photographers were usually on duty in addition to me. Each was given a clear assignment and had to photograph specific motifs for the marketing, sponsorship, and press departments. In addition to the cars, we also photographed the drivers, mechanics, engineers, and team boss. Everyone was, of course, clean and perfectly dressed, and ready for the shoot in the predefined time slot. During the two days and the night in between, all subjects were photographed. This resulted in autograph cards, press photos, posters, and images for advertising campaigns.

The creation of a 1967 analog autograph card for Jo Siffert.

The autograph and advertising logos were marked on a piece of tracing paper, which was placed over the black-and-white enlargement. Necessary image corrections were also marked on the tracing paper.

Jo Siffert

This was our highest-circulation autograph card ever. Tens of thousands of them were distributed. The portrait was taken at the prestart of the St. Ursanne–Les Rangiers hill climb in 1968.

I photographed Felipe Nasr and Marcus Ericsson during the first test session in Barcelona in 2016 for my last F1 autograph cards.

16 The Wild Pups

Little Money, Even Less Experience

Since young drivers have to make their mark, they often drive beyond their means. Not infrequently, the result is a pile of junk. It takes a great deal of talent to be able to compete at the front straightaway without a great deal of vehicle experience and track knowledge. Most of the time, there is a lack of time and money. In order to be able to climb the career ladder, a master's title is required by the second year at the latest. Unfortunately, the career of young drivers is increasingly dependent on a fat wallet.

Siffert's Premiere

In 1962, Jo Siffert entered his private Lotus 21 to qualify for the Monaco GP, firmly counting on the starting money. His failure to qualify was a slap in the face for him in two respects. Without a single franc in his pocket, he lamented his misfortune to my father. My father took pity on him and financed his return trip. The money was well invested. Seppi never forgot the help, and a friendship developed that lasted until Siffert's death.

Legendary pictures were taken of Clay Regazzoni's accident with the Tecno in the 1968 Monaco Formula 3 race. The Swiss driver lost control of the car in the harbor chicane and shot under the guardrail. Because the car's roll bar got stuck on the guardrail, it didn't fly into the sea. But in front of the bar is the driver's head. Miraculously, the man from Ticino climbed

out of the car on the outside of the guardrail, completely unharmed. The Reinhard pictures of this spectacular accident were shown again and again in the Swiss media. The same guardian angels allowed Romain Grosjean to survive in Bahrain 2020.

Brise: The Great Talent

Tony Brise was already considered a great talent when he collided with Alex Ribeiro in the Mirabeau in the 1975 Monaco Formula 3 race. That same year, he lined up for Graham Hill in the Embassy Hill Lola in Formula 1. On November 25 of the same year, Hill flew back to London from testing at Le Castellet in

◄ Clay Regazzoni managed to drive the Tecno F3 under the guardrail in 1968 and survive unharmed. The roll bar prevented the car from going into the water. Romain Grosjean achieved a similar feat in 2020 in Bahrain.

The Mirabeau was one of my father's favorite corners. When I traveled alone to the Monaco GP for the first time in 1980, he just said: "Go to the Mirabeau for the start; there's always something happening there."

his private plane, a twin-engine Piper Aztec, which he had bought with the victory bonus from Indianapolis. Also on the plane were Tony Brise, team manager Ray Brumble, designer Andy Smallman, and mechanics Tony Alcock and Terry Richards. In thick fog north of London, Hill grazed the treetops just before landing at Elstree airfield and crashed into a golf course near his home at Arkley. None of those on board survived the crash.

It was easier for photographers to get to know the lower-tier racing classes and younger drivers in person. The higher they go, the more difficult it is to get to them. For example, I got to know Markus Höttinger in the R5 Cup; Marc Surer in Formula 2; Michael Schumacher, Bernd Schneider, and Nick Heidfeld in Formula 3; and Sebastian Vettel and Nico Rosberg in Formula BMW. It's a great pleasure to follow these careers.

◀ + ▼ Tony Brise ended up on top of Alex Ribeiro in 1975. A year before, there was a pileup at the same place. Alessandro Pesenti-Rossi's Brabham came to rest with its left rear wheel in the cockpit of Tony Ruoff's GRD. A similar scene happened again in Monza 2021 with Max Verstappen and Lewis Hamilton. The only difference today is the HALO device, which offers enhanced protection for the drivers.

Pastor Maldonado became airborne at the GP2 race in Monza in 2010, but the incident had no consequences thanks to the greatly enhanced safety requirements of recent years.

145

Roberto Fillannino (number 18) provides a competitor with the launchpad for a flight into the unknown. This impressive picture was taken at the entrance to the Parabolica corner (Monza 1970) during the Formula Italia race, which was run with identical Fiat-Abarth racing cars. The later Formula BMW races were similar, but with BMW cars.

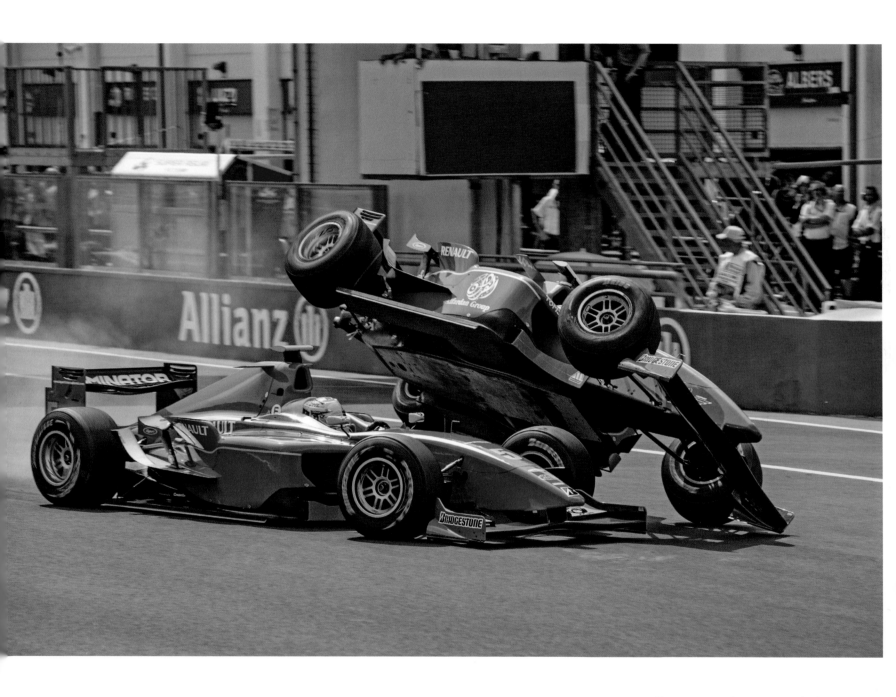

Teammates at close quarters. At the start of the Formula 3000 race in Magny-Cours in 2007, Andreas Zuber was taken to the cleaners by Timo Glock in the very first corner.

Graham Hill crashes the Brabham
BT 34 into the wall of the Tobacco
Corner in Monaco in 1971.

17 From Trademark to Filigree Work of Art

Helmets through the Years

Prior to the Second World War and into the 1950s, drivers wore short-sleeved polo shirts, normal everyday shoes, and simple gloves when racing. Before the war, a white dust cap served as head protection. Later this was replaced by a simple leather cap. The eyes were protected from wind and dirt by aviator goggles.

Without a Face

At the end of the 1950s, more and more drivers wore open helmets, aviator goggles with a drawstring, and a neck and mouth guard to protect against the wind. The head protection was held in place by a simple leather strap. To protect themselves from the sun, many drivers partially covered their goggles with adhesive tape.

Dan Gurney was the first to start with a full-face helmet in 1968. The mid-1970s model had a Velcro strap, a fireproof neck protector, and a hose that could deliver oxygen to the pilot in the cockpit in case of fire. With the integral helmet, however, the faces of the drivers had now suddenly disappeared. Since then, the only way to tell who was sitting in the car was by looking at the helmet design. Photographically, the contrast between the eyes in the darkness and the helmet suddenly had to be compensated for with a flash unit.

Recognition Feature

Over time, the helmet became a distinguishing feature and trademark of the driver. In historical photos, in the period from 1960 to the late 1990s, one can immediately tell who is in the car. Sir Stirling Moss once said, "I've had four helmets in my whole career; one is in Germany, I still own one, the remaining two were so broken I threw them away."

The white bars on Hill's dark blue helmet symbolize oar blades.

It was a long way from a simple cap to protect against dust, to the cool leather hood with aviator goggles and open-face helmets, to the safety works of art of the full-face helmets as we know them today.

A real branding strategy was maintained by the Hill family. Graham Hill raced all his life in dark blue headgear adorned with the typical white bars symbolizing oar blades. When his son Damon entered racing, he adopted his father's design. It must be remembered that, at that time, most drivers competed not only in Formula 1, but in various other categories as well. Graham Hill won across the board. To this day, he is the only one to have won the Triple Crown. This refers to his triumph at the Monaco GP, the 24 Hours of Le Mans, and the Indy 500. Because of his helmet, Hill is immediately recognizable in all the pictures of these victories, whether in the Lotus at the Indy 500 (1966), in the Matra-Simca at the 24 Hours of Le Mans (1972), or at Monaco (1963, 1964, 1965 in the BRM and 1968 and 1969 in the Lotus). Among others, Jackie Stewart in a Tyrrell or Chaparall, Jo Siffert in a BRM or Porsche, and John Surtees on the 500 cc MV Agusta or in the Honda RA300 V12 remained true to their trademark helmets.

Filigree Works of Art

In the late 1990s, Michael Schumacher began changing his helmet design every now and then. Sebastian Vettel went even further. I was able to take a picture of him with twelve different helmets worn by him in a single season. This makes it increasingly difficult to quickly identify the driver on the basis of a picture. Is that Vettel, or is it his teammate?

Technical advancements in paint application are allowing for ever-crazier helmet designs. There are no limits to creativity, and new, intricate works of art are often created within a few hours. For the young fan, this makes it increasingly difficult to compete in a soapbox or go-kart race in the helmet design of his great idol.

Damon Hill with his world championship helmet (*center*), flanked by those
worn by his father in the 1960s (*left*)
and 1970s (*right*)

A small, filigree work of art with flashing points of light was created especially for the Singapore Night Grand Prix. The company "JMD" (Jens Munser Design of Salzgitter) employs seven people, but Vettel's helmet is and remains a matter for the boss–after all, Sebastian has been a customer from the beginning. Since his karting days, he has been wearing head protection from JMD. Both Schumachers, as well as Webber, Barrichello, Rosberg, Massa, Ricciardo, and Verstappen, are, or were, numbered among the company's clientele.

◀▲ Nick Heidfeld displays helmets from his career. Blue and yellow predominate, but green and black also adorn the collection.

◀ Sebastian Vettel with the twelve helmets he wore during the 2012 season. Such a variety makes it difficult to quickly identify him when he is in the car.

Modern helmets (Nick Heidfeld in photo, 2009) have a carbon shell, are light (approx. 1,150 g or 40.6 oz.), and ventilated. In the past, the air was blown onto the driver's face, but now it's guided along the top of the head to the back, where it escapes again through vent holes.

155

18 Maximum Performance Up Until the Last Second

Pure Exhaustion

People often criticize motorsports as not being a top sport. "Anyone can drive around in circles," I hear time and again. The opposite is true. No driver can survive a GP without being in top shape. On the one hand, the centrifugal forces in the car are extremely high. In concrete terms, the drastic reduction in speed at the start of a corner puts up to 6 g of force on the driver's body (i.e., six times his weight). This puts extreme strain on the neck in particular. On the other hand, drivers have to maintain full concentration for around 100 minutes during a race. This is not easy when the track is wet or very hot. For example, a race driver loses up to 4 liters (4.2 quarts) of body fluids during a race in the heat. The heavy sweating is caused by the high temperatures in the car and the driver's fireproof overall. In total, a Formula 1 driver burns around 3,000 kilocalories during a race. So we're talking about real heavy labor here.

Collapse at the Finish Line

Ayrton Senna experienced just how much a Formula 1 race can push a driver to the physical limit at the 1992 San Marino Grand Prix at Imola. Completely exhausted, the Brazilian stopped his car just past the finish line and collapsed. I was on my way to the podium ceremony and saw Senna's McLaren stopped at the fence. I immediately ran over and took a picture through the chain-link fence with the wide-angle lens. His eyes closed, the Brazilian was in the cockpit being attended to by the doctor.

I ignored the annoying policeman next to me, who was trying to chase me away from the spot the whole time, and concentrated on my job. Then he started tugging at me. By now, I had my pictures in the can, so I was ready to clear the field. I turned around, and the long focal length that was on my shoulder gave the vigilante an unintentional-intentional blow to the head. With a friendly "Oh, scusi," I apologized and ran to the award ceremony.

Mental Blackout

On one occasion, I also reached the limits of my strength during a Formula 1 race. At the 2016 German Grand Prix in Hockenheim, I felt a thirst I'd never experienced before, even during the starting grid. During the race, I asked several colleagues for drinks. Nevertheless, my condition got worse and worse, and I finally had to throw up. At the exit of the Sachs curve, I went to see the track doctor. But he arrogantly turned me away. I collapsed on the way to the medical center. Mental blackout! Two colleagues then took me there. Only after the award ceremony did I regain consciousness, and I dragged myself to the media center. Under extremely difficult conditions, I sent the few pictures I had taken from there to my customers.

Cold shower for hot heads: Keke Rosberg and Nigel Mansell. Completely dehydrated, Nelson Piquet collapses during the award ceremony (1982 Brazilian GP). Keke Rosberg, with Sylvia, Nelson's girlfriend at the time, helps the unconscious winner back to his feet. Neither Piquet nor Rosberg have any idea that they will soon be disqualified because their cars were underweight; nor that Alain Prost, who is waiting in the picture, will be declared the winner of the race at the green table. Piquet later said, "I never accepted this disqualification; to me this is my twenty-fourth racing victory, and I still haven't given back the trophy."

At Imola in 1992, Ayrton Senna stopped immediately after the finish line with severe circulatory problems and required medical attention.

19 Helping and Dying for Racing

The Dangerous Life of the Track Marshal

Without marshals, there would be no motorsport. They control the racing action, warn the drivers by waving flags, provide important information to the race organizers, and help in the event of accidents. In short, they are the silent helpers in the second line. And there they are often exposed to great danger. Not only for the drivers, but also for us photographers, the marshal is an extremely important person. He's the one who decides on the spot. With his goodwill, photographic viewpoints at the limit of what is allowed are possible, or not. A comradely attitude is very helpful.

Deadly Fire Extinguisher

A track marshal was standing in the wrong place at the 1962 Monaco Grand Prix. Immediately after the start, a serious accident occurred as cars were braking for the Gasometer Hairpin corner. Richie Ginther, Ines Ireland, Maurice Trintignant, Trevor Taylor, and Dan Gurney collided with each other. A wheel came off Ginther's BRM and fatally struck a track marshal.

In 1977, an unthinkable accident involving a track marshal occurred at the South African Grand Prix at Kyalami. On the twenty-second lap, Renzo Zorzi had to park his Shadow on the left-hand side of the start-finish straightaway due to a defect and went to safety. Because his car caught fire, two marshals crossed the track. At the same time, Hans-Joachim

Stuck and Tom Pryce were racing toward the site of the breakdown, which they could not see for a long time because of a crest.

While Stuck managed to take evasive action, Pryce hit one of the two marshals at around 250 kilometers per hour (155 mph). The man was thrown through the air and died instantly. The fire extinguisher he was carrying struck Tom Pryce in the head, killing him as well. The now-driverless Shadow raced on at full throttle to the first turn. There it collided at full speed with the slowing Ligier driven by Jacques Laffite. The Frenchman escaped with a scare.

◀ A harmless starting collision involving five cars in Monaco in 1962 claimed the life of a track official in the background, who was struck and killed by a wheel that had come free.

A Maserati passes the sandbag-shielded helper, medical, and control post at the 1952 Swiss GP in Bern-Bremgarten.

Death after the End of the Race

A track helper first lost his radio, then his life.

While fatalities used to be part of racing, safety precautions improved from 1995 onward. At both Monza in 2000 and at Melbourne in 2001, a track marshal was killed by a flying wheel. After that, calm returned to Formula 1 until the Canadian Grand Prix in 2013. There, the Mexican Esteban Gutiérrez had to park his car shortly before the end of the race. After the subsequent finish by the winner Sebastian Vettel, fans stormed the track and ran toward the stranded Sauber Ferrari. In order to bring it to safety, the marshals began removing the car. While balancing the swinging race car on the hook of the moving tractor, a track marshal lost his radio. When he tried to pick it up, he fell and was run over by the rear tire of the recovery vehicle. Hours later, he succumbed to severe head injuries in the hospital.

I had photographed the scene and was fully focused on the Sauber hanging on the hook. Since the season so far had been anything but exhilarating for the Swiss racing team, the shot was intended to be emblematic of the team's poor performance. I didn't notice that I had also photographed the accident at the same time.

After the award ceremony, I immediately went to work. I selected the most important pictures and sent them to my customers. It wasn't until I finished that the negative headlines started coming through to me. Then, as the demand for just this one image grew, I realized that I had captured an event without knowing it and without wanting to. Of course, I immediately stopped further shipping of this image.

Years before, when analog pictures still had to undergo time-consuming processing, such a photo would never have reached the media.

> Then, as the demand for precisely this one image grew, I realized that I had captured an incident without knowing it and without wanting to.

Marshals monitor racing action around the globe on a voluntary basis. At the GP Europa at the Nürburgring, they also have a whistle.

Nothing is impossible! High-tech technology meets vintage cleaning equipment. Jarno Trulli (Toyota) after a collision with Takuma Sato at the Japanese GP at Suzuka in 2005.

Kyalami 1971, a situation similar to
the one that would claim two lives at
the same place six years later. A track
marshal crosses the lane in front of
Mario Andretti (Ferrari) to offer assistance to a driver who is in no danger.

▶ Image from the Spanish GP in
Barcelona, 2007

Bankruptcies, Bad Luck, and Breakdowns

All Good Things Come in Threes!

During practice for the 1,000-km (621-mile) race at Spa-Francorchamps in 1970, an incident occurred that is unimaginable today. Jo Siffert suffered a flat in the front left tire of his Porsche 917 on the Masta straight at 300 kilometers per hour (186 mph). Positive: the Swiss driver was able to bring the car to a halt unharmed. Negative: Although the sports prototypes of the time had to carry a spare wheel according to the regulations, this was of no use to the driver. To save weight, tools and jacks were not carried, and the spare wheel was not inflated. Only at the Targa Florio were these articles in the car, because the way to the pits could be extremely long.

Unlike today, at that time a breakdown vehicle did not immediately rush over, and the cell phone had not yet been invented. A longer wait was the order of the day. Then, all of a sudden, Finnish Porsche colleague Leo Kinnunen showed up in the spare 917 with an inflated spare wheel, jack, and tools. But the wheel nut was so jammed that the tool wrench bent in all directions due to the high pressure. Kinnunen had to take his 917 back to the pits for a replacement. Back on-site, the wheel could finally be changed and both cars set off again.

Unbelievably (but true), the same story repeated itself just a few minutes later. The same driver was involved in exactly the same place, again with a flat in the left front tire. The only small difference: the first time "Seppi" stopped the Gulf-Porsche on the left side of the track, the second time on the right side. Once again, Leo Kinnunen came to provide "roadside assistance," and this time the wheel change was completed on the first attempt.

When Brian Redman later picked up the team's third flat, the mechanics roughened the insides of the rims overnight. This was to prevent the tire from wandering on the rim, which had been identified as the cause of the triple flat. The happy ending followed the next day: the Porsche with start number 24 (Siffert/Redman) won the race by just under three minutes, ahead of the Ferrari duo Jacky Ickx and John Surtees.

Those were the last years when a photographer was often the only witness on-site. He alone brought the pictures home and could sell them for a good fee. The race distances became shorter and more visible over the years, so that today, all special situations are captured three- and fivefold, from various directions.

20 Genius on Four Wheels

Walter Röhrl: The Always-Calm Perfectionist

When asked who was the more complete racing driver, the rally driver or the circuit pilot, the surprising answer came from three-time Le Mans winner Marco Werner: "Walter Röhrl!" In fact, the driver from Regensburg is still considered the measure of all things, even among much younger racing drivers. Again and again, he achieved top positions in various vehicles: in the Opel Ascona 400, in the Fiat 131 Abarth, in the Lancia Rallye 037, in the Group B Audi Sport Quattro at the rallies, in the Lancia Beta Montecarlo at endurance races, in the Trans-Am or IMSA Audi, in the DTM Audi V8 Quattro, and in the Porsche 935 on the circuit. Röhrl was the complete racing driver who mastered both rally and circuit racing.

The sayings of the extremely likable Bavarian are also legendary: "A car is only fast enough when you stand in front of it in the morning and are afraid to unlock it." Or, "When accelerating, the tears of emotion must flow horizontally toward the ear." And, "If you see the tree you're driving into, you have understeer. If you only hear it, you have oversteer." About a special stage at the Monte-Carlo Rally, he says, "It was snowing heavily and I had to drive first. With 20 centimeters (7.9 inches) of fresh snow, you're a snowplow and snow groomer in one, so you're usually minutes slower. I drove 30 kilometers (18.6 miles) beyond good and evil. You couldn't see where the road ended and where the abyss was, and I drove six seconds faster than Stig Blomquist. Normally, he should have been two minutes faster . . . that was certainly the best special test of my life."

Without Drama

Working with Walter Röhrl is always a pleasure. Even today, he wants to know exactly where I will press the shutter release, so that he can set the perfect scene for the car at that particular spot.

Walter Röhrl walking along the road. His motto was to go into the race well prepared, especially in conditions of poor visibility. "The Tall One" then became a "traveling navigation system," such as on the "Night of the Long Knives" at the 1986 Monte Carlo Rally.

Walter Röhrl also drove the Fiat Panda
4x4 to its limits, as we witnessed during a
Sport Auto shoot in the 1990s.

I'll never forget a *Sport Auto* shoot at Saalbach Hinterglemm. Walter Röhrl and Keke Rosberg were testing the 4×4 cars of the time: from the Fiat Panda to the Lancia Delta Integrale. The vehicles were lined up on an icy mountain road. I was missing only the final picture. Therefore, I waited for twilight. As always in photo shoots with narrow space conditions, at the stupidest moment a road user came along. When he saw the cars, he thought it was a traffic blockade caused by a few morons. Cursing, the approaching farmer tried to stop his car on the ice-covered road. But he failed. The car kept moving, and at the same time, the driver began to shout insults at us from the open side window. Gradually, we realized that the sliding car was inevitably going to hit one of our test vehicles. In response to Keke Rosberg's statement, "I don't think this is going to be good," Walter calmly strode toward the still-sliding vehicle. From the outside, he reached through the side window, grasped the steering wheel, and instructed the visibly surprised driver, "So, now release the brake. I just told you not to brake. Now, brake very gently. Not so hard. Yes, just like that." Walter walked along with the baffled farmer and skillfully steered his car past the test vehicles. Afterward, he bid him a friendly farewell.

And Always Perfect

When looking at photos in magazines, he was never interested in whether the shot was a good one. It was more important to him that the picture expressed driving perfection. If not, he was quick to say what the driver could have done better. When asked which shots still evoked a "Wow!" experience for him, he said, "All the ones where the car is transverse, but the front wheels are pointing straight ahead. There's a picture of that in the Fiat 131 Abarth at the 1980 Monte Carlo Rally on snow in a downhill left turn, or one from 1984 on the Col de Turini in the long Quattro."

As with most racing drivers, for Walter Röhrl the personal significance of photos increases with age. "For me, they're a great trip back in time."

At the Saalbach Classic, Walter Röhrl showed the participants his incredible skills every year—like here in 2017 in the Heigo Porsche on gravel.

At the 1998 Planai-Classic, Röhrl
even competed against a fast horse
on the Gröbming, driving a prewar
MG Kompressor.

Although Röhrl never really liked "driving in circles," in 1980 he and Riccardo Patrese started in various brand world championship races in the Lancia Beta Montecarlo Turbo, often making the Italian despair of his lap times. Three podium places, the victory at Brands Hatch, a second place in Mugello with team colleague Alboreto, and third place at Monza on April 27, 1980 (pictured here) underscored his ability.

Severe water damage at the Röhrls' home delayed this photo shoot by hours, but then he really let rip with the Audi.

Walter Röhrl waits at his workplace in the Group
B Audi Quattro (1986) for the next race. Christian
Geistdörfer is in the hot seat still studying the
"prayer book."

Walter, the gifted speaker, as he is known and loved today

21 Silent Heroes

Who Remembers the Lifesavers?

From the 1960s through the late 1970s, fire was the racing driver's most dangerous enemy. Back then, the racing car, which could reach speeds of up to 300 kilometers per hour (186 mph), was actually a mobile bomb. It consisted of over 200 liters (53 gallons) of gasoline and the glowing hot exhaust manifolds that served as the igniter. Even if the driver was not injured in a crash, the subsequent fire could still result in death. Trapped in their cockpits, Jo Siffert, Lorenzo Bandini, Pedro Rodriguez, Piers Courage, Roger Williamson, Jo Schlesser, and many others lost their lives. Niki Lauda and Clay Regazzoni would also have been killed, if it hadn't been for the true heroes of the sport.

Fight against the Flames

The world champions are all known, even in order, but the lifesavers are hardly known at all. Many remember Niki Lauda's fiery crash at the Nürburgring in 1976. There, the small, lanky Italian asphalt cowboy Arturo Merzario left no stone unturned, and in the end, he managed to pull the already badly burned Lauda out of the cockpit. With this action, he saved his life. Five years earlier, in the 1,000-kilometer race in Buenos Aires, he had failed in a similar attempt. Merzario was unable to pull his teammate Ignazio Giunti out of his Ferrari. The flames were too fierce. Mike Hailwood saved Clay Regazzoni's life at the

1973 South African GP at Kyalami. After an accident involving him, Jackie Ickx, and Clay Regazzoni, the Swiss driver remained seated in his burning BRM. The Englishman immediately recognized the dangerous situation and pulled the unconscious Regazzoni out of the cockpit. Thanks to Hailwood, the Swiss driver was taken to hospital with only a few burns.

"I'm Paid to Drive"

Tragedy struck at Zandvoort on July 29, 1973. David Purley alone tried frantically to rescue the injured driver Roger Williamson from his burning March 731. All the other drivers continued the race. Lap

◀ Roger Williamson lost his life in an accident in his March on July 29, 1973. The clouds of black smoke rising from behind the dunes at Zandvoort are the visible sign of this tragedy.

David Purley tried to come to the aid of his colleague, but his heroic effort against the fire was unsuccessful.

after lap, they raced past the dying Williamson. Meanwhile, Purley was fighting the flames. But he had no chance. The only fire extinguisher on-site wasn't working properly, and the marshals didn't have fireproof clothing. They had to watch right next to the March as the British driver burned to death. The sad thing was that the TV pictures of Purley's one-sided fight against the fire were broadcast live to living rooms all over the world. Worryingly, at the finish line Lauda said into the microphone, "I'm paid to drive, not to park!"

Today, the live broadcasts lag behind the ongoing events by a few seconds. This gives the director time to react in the event of an accident, such as the one involving Romain Grosjean in Bahrain in 2020, and switch to other cameras. If the accident proves to be harmless, it can be shown later.

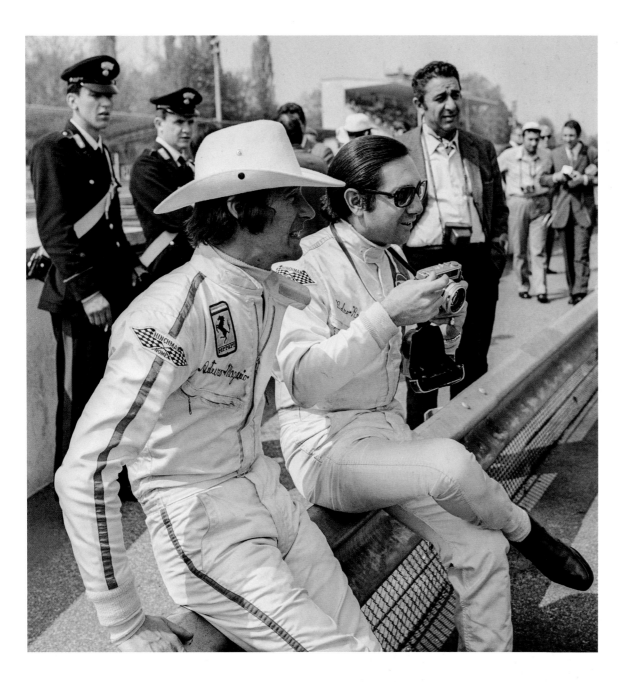

Like Roger Williamson, Piers Courage also fell victim to the flames at Zandvoort on June 21, 1970. Mike Hailwood rescued Clay Regazzoni from his burning BRM at Kyalami in 1973. A deep friendship developed between the two. Rescuer and victim: Arturo Merzario (with the obligatory cowboy hat), who saved Niki Lauda's life, talking to Mexican Pedro Rodriguez (with camera), for whom all help came too late after his car caught fire following an accident at the Norisring on July 11, 1971.

22 "Dani's Messed Up the Picture"

A Good Start Picture Is Half the Battle

Fellow professional photographer Yves Debraine summed up the photographer's excitement just before the start back in the early 1960s: "Nine minutes until the start. I'll stand a little farther to the left; that's better! Seven minutes before the start, but I can't believe it; there's a cloud coming. Five minutes to go. This guy is not going to get in front of me now! Three minutes to go. I wonder if I shouldn't have moved to the other side of the road. Two minutes to go. The cloud is there and steals two apertures from me. One minute to go until the start: 'You can't stand here; it's too dangerous,' says a marshal. Since the engines are already roaring, I turn a deaf ear and gaze spellbound into the viewfinder. They start, full concentration on the focus. So NOW . . . CLICK . . . but only after the film is developed will I know if the pictures turned out well."

Until the end of the 1950s, cameras had to be operated completely manually. The film had to be advanced after each shot, and the mechanical shutter had to be recocked. Only then could another image be captured. Each photographer therefore only ever had one chance to take a good start picture. As soon as the cars were in the predetermined focus, the exposure was taken. If an accident occurred outside the intended image area, the photographer was out of luck. Under these conditions, there was a great risk of having an out-of-focus or totally blurred image of the start. If an accident happened after the first exposure, one had a second chance. In the meantime, one could cock the shutter, manually adjust the focus, and press the release one more time. Only after the film had been developed did it become clear whether the pictures had been successful. The legendary Nikon F was launched in 1959 and was the first camera with a motor. This massively facilitated the work of photographers. In the years that followed, the devices underwent a great deal of further development. The invention of autofocus, which enables the camera to automatically focus on the subject, at the end of the 1970s was a milestone in sports photography. Today, up to ten images per second are possible. This makes our job massively easier. However, technological progress also contributes to the fact that there is hardly any individuality in the photographers' shots.

Increased Safety Regulations

Since the introduction of Formula 1, something has remained the same: the start is still the main photographic motif of every race, no matter what happens in the subsequent 100 minutes. With a good picture of the start, the photographer has reaped half the rewards.

Unfortunately, starts have lost a lot of their drama in recent years due to the much wider start-finish straightaways. Today, the twenty or so cars look more like toys on an oversized parking lot, and the distances between the vehicles are far too great from a photographic point of view. In addition, in contrast to the past, the tires and engines produce almost no smoke. As well, today the racing cars start in staggered rows

The first of about 700 F1 start pictures taken by the two Reinhards was shot at the Swiss Grand Prix in Bern on June 4, 1950.

Smoke and fumes add a great deal of drama to this picture of the start of the 1970 South African GP at Kyalami, with pole sitter Jackie Stewart in the March taking the lead.

of two. Until 1974, the starting rows consisted of three, two, and then again three cars that started side by side.

The photo areas have also changed a lot. In the past, photographers, including my father, could photograph the start directly from the edge of the track. They had no protection, either from a guardrail or from a barrier. Pictures from the pit wall were also allowed. Today that is impossible. The pit wall is closed to everyone during the start, including the team bosses and team managers. Think of the momentum a crash can develop. Entire cars or individual parts quickly fly through the air in all directions and become dangerous projectiles.

Today, photographers have to position themselves far away from the starting line on the racetrack, protected behind the runoff zone and the safety fence. This illustrates the great danger under which some of the historic racing photographs were taken. At the same time, it is not surprising that the pictures of that time convey much more drama and excitement.

Wire Cutters

At Imola, one year after Ayrton Senna's fatal accident in 1994, the fast Tamburello curve was converted into a slow chicane. The first braking point after the start was located there; a great spot from which to take photos. But unfortunately, the fence was in the way. The responsible FIA representative refused our request for a photo window. There were three of us standing behind the fence. At that time, a good pair of wire cutters belonged in every photographer's vest. So we cut the hole out of the fence ourselves and took pictures. On Monday, we found we were in trouble with the FIA in Paris. The track marshal had given us away! Our penalty: at the next race in Barcelona, Bernie Ecclestone took away our permanent accreditations. At least we were given a simple cardboard pass as a replacement and were able to do our job. At the same time, it meant the end of the wire cutters for us photographers.

Vettel Too Fast

Throughout the 2011 season, Sebastian Vettel in the Red Bull pulled ahead of his opponents at the start. He usually had a large lead after just a few meters. The problem: because of this fast start, if I wanted to photograph the field in the first chicane after the start, half the cars were not in the picture. I was annoyed about this situation and said to Sebastian, "Do you know that your super starts are ruining our start pictures?" In response to his inquiries, I explained the problem to him. Vettel understood what I was

The front row of the starting grid—
Jochen Rindt, Jackie Stewart, and
Dennis Hulme—takes off at the 1969
British Grand Prix at Silverstone.

An incredible crowd follows the Indianapolis 500 every year. In the "front row" for the 1991 Indy 500 were Rick Mears, AJ Foyt, and Mario Andretti.

▶▲ Swiss Grand Prix, Bern-Bremgarten 1950.

▶ Wolfgang Count Berghe von Trips in the Ferrari 246P (7), next to Joachim Bonnier (4) and Hans Herrmann (5), both in Porsche 718/2s

saying, but didn't promise me any improvement. Shortly afterward, he once again won the European GP in Valencia in a highly superior manner. When I congratulated him on the victory, he said, "I thought of you after the first chicane." "How so?" I replied. The Red Bull driver then said, "When I looked in the rearview mirror and saw my lead, I immediately realized: Oh shit! Now I've probably ruined Dani's start picture again." That is indeed what happened.

The Missed Start

At the Indianapolis 500, it was always a major struggle to even get a picture of the start.

The grandstands were closed to photographers, and the assigned photo spots for nonhouse Indy photographers didn't offer a direct view of the start-finish straight. So once I sneaked into the grandstand very early before the race. There, I looked for the best spot and asked the fans if I could photograph the start from the ground between their feet. Being Swiss, I was an exotic and got certain privileges with the fans. And so they not only offered me the spot but also provided me with beer. For a long time, I calmly remained in my position. But only two minutes before the start, a marshal spotted me and ordered me out of there. The clamor of the fans to leave me alone got so out of hand that in the end, half of the grandstand missed the start. Of course, my film also remained unexposed.

The start of the Italian Grand Prix at Monza in 1968.
John Surtees in the Honda starts from pole position. From
today's perspective, it's unbelievable how many people are on
the track during the start.

◀ Swiss Grand Prix at Bern-Bremsgarten in 1954 (*top*),
French Grand Prix at Reims in 1966 (*middle*),
German Grand Prix at Nürburgring in 1968 (*bottom*)

For every driver, each start can be his last. On September 10, 1961, at Monza, Wolfgang Count Berghe von Trips started from the pole position in the Ferrari 156, the so-called Sharknose, with start number 4. He had a fatal accident on the second lap following a collision with Jim Clark. His out-of-control Ferrari also took the lives of fifteen spectators. It is, and, one hopes, will remain, the worst accident in F1 history.

The start lights count up the five double lights, one every second, and when they go out, the race begins. Here, at Shanghai in 2010, the field waits at high revs for the signal to start.

In 2005, Charlie Whiting waits for the man with the green flag at the end of the field to indicate that the last competitor has come to a halt, then he presses the green button to start the start timer. I was the first to be able to take this picture at that time. I wasn't in the tower when the photo was taken. The camera was mounted under FIA supervision before the race and then remotely triggered. The first attempt at the Hungarian Grand Prix failed because of an interruption in the radio link.

▶ At the end of a long weekend, only the tire marks on the asphalt bear witness to what happened.

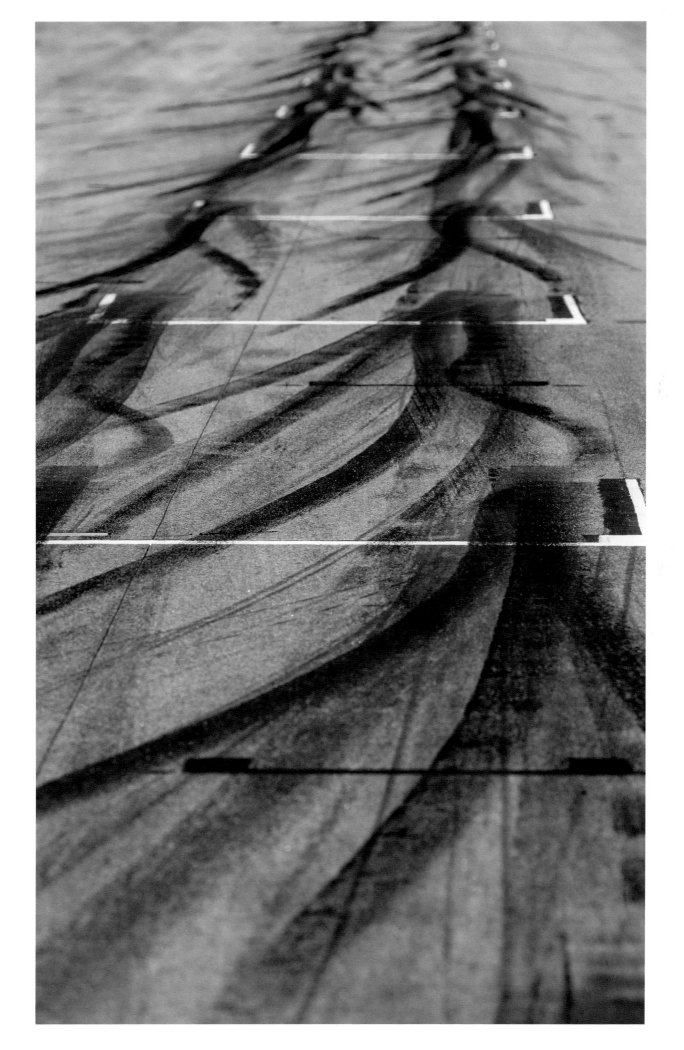

Yawning emptiness in all the grandstands for the start of the German Touring Car Masters at the Euro-Speedway in Lausitz in 2020 testify to the effects of the coronavirus pandemic.

◀ A full house at Le Mans in 1970 where, after various protests, the "Le Mans start"—in which the drivers ran across the track, got in, and started their cars—was abolished. At the front is the Porsche 917L of Vic Elford and Kurt Ahrens.

23 Wing Salad

Not Every Technical Innovation Was a Success

On May 4, 1969, at the Spanish Grand Prix, there were fourteen cars at the starting line. All of them were adorned with high wings. What was the reason for this wing clutter? The year before, the Chaparral 2F had competed in the sports prototype category for the first time with a gigantic wing. Shortly thereafter, Ferrari also successfully used a wing at the Belgian Grand Prix. Now, in the new season, all the teams were suddenly competing with these aerodynamic aids. The airfoils were even movable, setting themselves flat on the straight and steep when braking for the corner. However, the undulating track at the Circuit de Montjuïc in Barcelona, with its crest where the race cars lifted off slightly, was the undoing of this difficult technology.

"At the Start, Everything Was Still Going Well . . ."

At the start, everything went well. Rindt confidently defended the pole position and took a clear lead in the Lotus 49B. Teammate Graham Hill battled with Jo Siffert (Lotus) and Chris Amon (Ferrari) for eight laps before he was able to leave them behind. The first crash followed just one lap later: the wing on Graham Hill's Lotus broke at around 230 kilometers per hour (143 mph), just before the aforementioned

crest. The car first hit the guardrail on the left, then on the right, and came to a halt just before the hairpin after a slide of more than 150 meters (492 feet). Hill climbed out of the wreckage unhurt, watched the race from the side of the track, and saw that the wing on Jochen's car was not going to last much longer either. Using hand signals, he tried to draw his teammate's attention to this, but without success. The

German-Austrian Jochen Rindt takes his seat in his Lotus and starts from pole position for the Spanish GP on Mont-juïc, one of Barcelona's two local mountains. In addition to the Grand Prix, the city also hosted the World's Fair (1929) and the Summer Olympics (1992).

second crash followed just ten laps later: Rindt delivered an exact copy of Hill's accident at the same spot. After two guardrail contacts, however, the Lotus struck his teammate's car like a bomb, the latter acting like a ski jump. Rindt's car took off and rolled over. The German-Austrian was extremely lucky. He only broke his nose in this terrible accident and suffered a few bruises.

"Disaster Sepp" Was There

My father was positioned just behind the crest, holding the Hasselblad with its 500mm telephoto lens just above the guardrail. There, he photographed the slightly jumping cars and had the optimal location when suddenly Hill slid across the road with his bent wing. Thus "Disaster Sepp" once again lived up to his name. When the debris started flying, he ducked behind the planking. Nevertheless, part of the Lotus hit the sun visor on his lens. It crumpled like a piece of paper. My father tried in vain to remove the wrecked lens. Without success. He had to put the Hasselblad aside and switch to the Nikon. A few laps later, the wing of Jochen's Lotus also buckled, and the Lotus flew over his teammate's car. The result is a crazy picture that shows the enormous forces generated by the collision.

Question of Trust

The Spanish Grand Prix was a crazy race. Just six cars crossed the finish line. Jochen Rindt, who had taken pole position and subsequently became a victim of the new wing, said after the race, "Lotus always wants to go faster. But people forget that the cars have to make it to the end." And when asked by a reporter if he had lost confidence in his Lotus after the accident, he said, "I never had any!" The new wings were banned after the Spanish GP. From then on, it was stated that downforce-producing surfaces had to be part of the bodywork and could not extend above the roll bar.

◀+▼▼ Graham Hill loses control of his Lotus after the failure of the wing supports and slams into the guardrail.

The visibly shaken Hill tried to warn his teammate, but Rindt also flew off the track and struck the wreckage of the Briton's car.

24 Trofeo Lorenzo Bandini

Award for Outstanding Performance

My father witnessed a terrible accident at the GP Monaco on May 7, 1967. Near the harbor chicane, he had to watch as Lorenzo Bandini got stuck in a Ferrari that was ablaze. Only after three minutes did the track marshals manage to pull the thirty-one-year-old driver out of the car. Three days later, Bandini succumbed to his serious injuries.

In 1992, Bandini's sister established the Trofeo Lorenzo Bandini. This honors young racing drivers who have distinguished themselves with great performances in the past season. The first winner was Ivan Capelli. Sebastian Vettel received the award in 2009. The decisive factor was his outsider victory in the Toro Rosso at the 2008 rain race at Monza. Since the award ceremony also honors a journalist or photographer for their services to motorsport, I was able to accept the Trofeo Lorenzo Bandini from his sister together with my friend Sebastian in Brisighella (Emilia Romagna). Later, there was a fantastic dinner. Sitting at the same table with people such as Nino Vaccarella, Arturo Merzario, Gerhard Berger, and Sebastian Vettel was simply a unique experience for me.

◀▲ Lorenzo Bandini (Ferrari 158) in the Parabolica Corner at Monza, 1964

◀▼ The Ferrari 312 F1, completely burned out after the accident in Monaco in 1967

The author with Sebastian Vettel at the tribute in Brisighella

◀ In 2008, Polish driver Robert Kubica was honored with the Trofeo Lorenzo Bandini as Rookie of the Year. BMW didn't want to just send him to the award ceremony on foot but had the idea that he should be the first winner to pick up the prize in an F1 car. I was driven ahead in a BMW 3 series convertible by team manager Beat Zehnder to take pictures from the car on the unusual ride. We in turn were escorted by two police motorcycles with blue lights. To our astonishment, the road from Faenza to Brisighella was not closed off, but only the two escorting policemen directed the traffic to the side. Since an F1 is not built for slow driving and needs a certain airflow for cooling, our ride was really brisk through the traffic. Almost all the other motorists assumed that our convertible was the vehicle being escorted by the police, and of course did not expect in the slightest that a real Formula 1 could come along. Of course, due to its low height, it could hardly be seen in the rearview mirror. Kubica squeezed through the noisy road users, some of whom simply drove wildly to the right or left into the greenery.

▲ Sebastian Vettel also drove the same route in the Toro Rosso the following year, with the slight difference that everything was now neatly cordoned off.

Even Peter Sauber Was Amazed: The Relationship between the Dollar and the Franc

There is only one currency in Formula 1: the dollar. All teams from outside the dollar region have to convert their costs into dollars and are exposed to currency fluctuations. To illustrate the differences between the individual currencies, I came up with the idea for a picture using an old pharmacist's scale. I was able to get the scale quickly and easily from the pharmacist. The money, however, was another matter. So I went to the regional bank in Sarnen. There I asked a colleague who worked there for about 15,000 dollars and maybe 5,000 francs to realize my picture idea. I explained the details to him. After thinking it over for a short time, he spontaneously gave me his consent. He went into the safe, and I was loaned the money for about twenty-four hours without any exchange fees, account numbers, or paperwork. At Peter Sauber's office, I put the scales on the table, pulled thousands of dollars and francs out of my pocket, and placed them on the two weighing pans. Peter's eyes widened and he asked me where I had gotten all that money. I said, "I just borrowed it," and told him the story. This astonished him, and he replied, "Out there in the country where you are, such things can still happen. Here in the city, you wouldn't stand a chance."

Unusual image ideas are usually associated with effort and organization, and the environment must also play along.

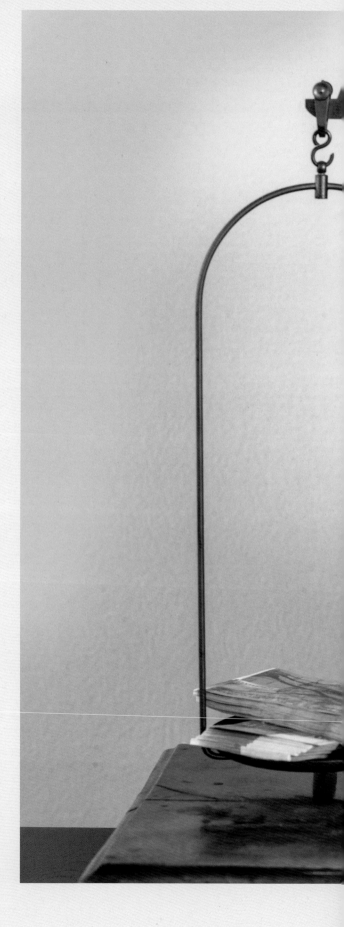

25 Schumacher's Name in My Medical Record

Photographers Live Dangerously

As a photographer, I lived dangerously even though the safety conditions improved year by year. During my career, I was really lucky three times. Chronologically, the first was the 1,000-kilometer (621-mile) race at Monza in 1984, where the Argentine Oscar Larrauri lost control of his Brun-Porsche 956 while braking for the first chicane. The car plowed across the grass toward the guardrail, directly toward me. Trying to run was pointless. The conditions were too tight. So I decided to take a few final photos. Equipped with the Pentax 6 × 7 cm medium-format camera and the 400mm telephoto lens, I had the chance to take two sharp pictures, because the car was in focus only twice—once before and once after hitting the guardrail. In between, I had to mechanically advance the film. If the Porsche had flown over the knee-high guardrail, I would have had a real problem.

At the 1993 Formula 3000 race at Spa, I needed the protection of a second guardian angel when I was standing at the exit of the Bus Stop chicane with my Japanese colleague Norio Koike and a race car slammed into the guardrail in front of our lenses. Our attempts to take pictures failed because the optics were much too long. I didn't realize that a severed wheel and suspension flew at me from above and hit the ground just 2 meters (6.6 feet) away. Norio looked at me and said dryly, "Lucky boy!"

That wheel would have killed me for sure. Two drivers were less fortunate: both Austrian Markus Höttinger (1980) and John Surtees's son Henry (2009) were killed by flying wheels.

I had to get to safety during the 1994 DTM race at the Norisring after the brake disc on Keke Rosberg's Opel Calibra failed while braking for the Grundig corner. At the end of the long full-throttle straight, the Finn sped into the runoff zone completely unbraked. We photographers were still allowed to stand there at the time. At the last moment, I managed to jump to the side. When the Opel Calibra came to a halt, Rosberg got out and made sure that nothing had happened to me. Many years later, when Keke's son Nico was already driving a Mercedes, we met in the passenger terminal of the airport in Qatar and had a burger together. I mentioned the accident, and Keke immediately remembered the photographer he had flown toward. He didn't remember that I was that photographer. But he said that it was a load off his mind when he saw the person in front of him in one piece.

Knocked Out by a Billboard

The now-much narrower and also slower Remus Curve at Spielberg used to be called the Bosch Curve and was one of the absolutely insane curves in Formula 1. The cars exited this opening 180-degree corner at over 250 kilometers per hour (155 mph). With only a triple guardrail between us and the track, we were able to photograph the action. When Nelson Piquet's Brabham hit the guardrail in practice, I ducked low to the ground and felt the violent impact, as well as

Without my guardian angel, I would have been killed by this detached front wheel at Spa in 1993.

Nelson got out of the car unharmed, but an unconscious photographer was lying next to me. I began to tend to him. Fortunately, he soon regained consciousness.

Schumacher in My Medical File

In 2000, I suffered a painful foot injury at the British Grand Prix at Silverstone. Michael Schumacher was on the grid ahead of his brother Ralf. I was kneeling and taking pictures of Ralf getting out of his Williams BMW when Michael pulled up behind me and hit my foot with his left rear wheel. Michael got out of his Ferrari immediately, came over, and said to me, "I was hoping it was one of the paparazzi. But I'm really sorry that it was you I hit. Are you okay?" I didn't feel much at the moment. I went on to photograph the race, and I flew home that evening with pain slowly making itself felt. The next morning came the rude awakening. I couldn't get out of bed. Since it was Easter Monday, I could not visit my family doctor, Dr. Urs Wipfli. Instead, I had to go to one of his colleagues and ended up with Dr. Josef Jeker. He wanted to know exactly what had happened to my swollen foot. I told him that he would not believe the truth. At his insistence, I said, "Michael Schumacher ran over me with his Ferrari yesterday!" Dr. Jeker started laughing loudly and said that was the best thing he had ever heard. Then I was able to tell him the truth, which is exactly what I did.

And so to this day, Michael Schumacher remains in my medical file as the cause of my foot injury.

With motion blur as a result of my flight to avoid Keke Rosberg's Opel Calibra, a final image emerged of him flying toward me unbraked and at high speed into the runoff zone.

the subsequent slide by the car. When everything was quiet again, I stood up and looked to see what had happened. Nelson was already getting out of the car unharmed, but next to me was an unconscious photographer. I started to take care of him. Fortunately, he came around after a short time. The crazy thing was that he hadn't been hit by any part of the vehicle, but while trying to get to safety, he had run headlong into the huge billboard just behind us.

Rosberg, red-faced, explains that he almost ran over the photographer back there.

In the days before autofocus, the out-of-control Porsche 956 was in focus exactly twice—once in front of me and once behind me—but in between, the film had to be advanced manually.

26 Manhattan

New York, New York

. . . is the title song from Martin Scorsese's 1977 film of the same name: "I want to wake up in the city that never sleeps, and feel like I'm the king of the hill! Top of the heap! Boss of the whole bunch! King of this hill!" The cover version by Frank Sinatra in 1979 brought the song world fame, while Scorsese's film flopped.

My days in New York were exciting and impressive. Several times, I photographed exciting stories in Manhattan with different Formula 1 faces. Since the races in Indianapolis and Canada (Montreal) took place within a week, there were three days to visit the US metropolis. Jean Todt took the opportunity to look around the US art scene, Gerhard Berger was sent by Benetton to the city, and Juan Pablo Montoya was a guest on David Letterman's show.

In 1997, we wanted to spend three pleasant days in New York with Gerhard Berger. But things turned out differently. Already on the first day, Berger was paralyzed by an acute episode of maxillary sinusitis, which causes severe toothache. In search of a doctor, we drove the hotel limousine all over Manhattan. We used the time for Michael Schmidt to conduct his planned interview with Berger. When he arrived at the doctor, he found that the maxillary sinusitis came from the inflamed ethmoid—a bone of the skull, which is located at the end of the nasal cavity on the edge of the cranial cavity. Berger was given antibiotics. Back at the hotel, the Formula 1 driver watched the photo shoot in hellish pain. Flavio Briatore, his Benetton team boss at the time, called him and asked about his well-being. Briatore quickly added that he had spoken to the attending physician and that a start in Canada was probably out of the question. It is far too dangerous to drive with antibiotics.

Considering the circumstances, Berger flew home and was treated in the hospital. Then his father had an accident, and so he stayed away from the GP France

Once high above the streets and once deep in the urban canyons of Manhattan. Gerhard Berger, who was plagued by a toothache, happened to find a suitable motif in the skyscrapers, while Ferrari's team boss Jean Todt stood on the street at dusk.

At the request of Nicola Bulgari, his "Woody" was photographed in front of the newly opened shop on 5th Avenue, which led to a considerable traffic obstruction.

and England. It was only years later that it became clear why the retirement of the Tyrolean came at an opportune time for the Benetton team boss. Briatore had already signed a contract for three races with Alexander Wurz at the beginning of the season. Briatore had been trying all season to get rid of Jean Alesi, and now, fortunately, Gerhard Berger had to pass for three races. This story came to light because Alexander Wurz's manager did not pay his starting fee, and Briatore took him to court.

By the way, at Hockenheim, Berger reported back in the cockpit and showed everyone why he was the champion. After taking the pole position, he won the race ahead of Michael Schumacher and also set the fastest race lap.

Just one week after 9/11 in 2001, the Italian GP was held. Ferrari showed grief for the first and only time. Both F-1 cars wore matte black noses and remained free of all advertising inscriptions. After the death of the company founder Enzo Ferrari on August 14, 1988, the racing cars had worn a simple mourning ribbon in the following two races at the Belgian GP and at the home race in Monza. But the attack on the World Trade Center in New York changed everything.

A year later, I was back in New York with Juan Pablo Montoya. The Colombian was a guest on David Letterman's late-night show. Of course, we also visited Ground Zero to get an idea of the extent of the terrorist attack. Arriving in the makeup room of the TV studio, Juan Pablo was prepared for the interview with David Letterman. Of course, it was planned that I could photograph the driver during the show. But I never actually got out of the makeup room . . .

I was also in New York with Jean Todt in 2002. The then-Ferrari team boss and later FIA president visited various art studios, and I was responsible for the recording the visit. For me, it was a special event. The art scene in New York is huge, and under normal circumstances, it wouldn't have been so easy to get an insight into these extremely interesting work-spaces. Todt is a huge devotee of modern art. At his home, he had a collection of about forty pictures. "Unfortunately, I can't afford classical paintings," Todt laughed in Manhattan.

A very special photo job led me to New York in 1996. I had been allowed to visit the vehicle collection of the then vice president of the House of Bulgari, Nicola Bulgari, in Rome. Impressed by my work, he then sent me to the US to photograph the remaining cars in his collection. Having a photographic record of his cars was enormously important to him. He really wanted to have his "Woody" photographed on 5th Avenue in front of his shop. Early in the morning—before sunrise and before all the traffic had blocked the roads—the rare 1942 Buick Special Estate Wagon was delivered to the trailer and placed directly in front of the shop. I had only a few minutes left to capture the unique situation on film without much trouble.

In all these decades, Ferrari wore mourning at the 2001 Italian GP only one time, with a matte black nose mourning ribbon–following the terrorist attacks on 9/11.

▶▲ Juan Pablo Montoya waits for his interview in the makeup room of David Letterman's late-night show.

▶ Jean Todt–as always on the telephone–admires the modern art of Peter Halley (*far right*).

▶▶ An officer on Schumacher Way in Indianapolis

. . . the Car with Michael Schumacher or Nelson Piquet

As a motorsport photographer, over time you build up a relationship of trust and sometimes even friendship with some of the drivers. Over the years, I have been chauffeured by many famous drivers. Each time, I was fascinated by their incredible mastery of the vehicle. They accelerate quickly, stay far away from the grass, and pull their cars around the curves as if on rails.

Crash with Udo Jürgens

Berghe Count von Trips showed my father the correct steering wheel position in a VW Beetle back in 1960. And he still dreams of his ride with John Surtees in the Ferrari 250 LM at Reims. His favorite story is about his cab ride after the Dutch Grand Prix in 1969. To this day, the drive from Zandvoort is extremely time consuming and involves a lot of traffic jams. In order to get to the airport more quickly, my father hitched a ride to Amsterdam Schipol in a rental car driven by Jo Siffert. Shortly before, the Swiss racing driver had taken an excellent second place behind Jackie Stewart. Since time was short, Siffert took a shortcut and drove a few hundred meters along the sandy beach before heading back up the embankment onto the road with a little too much momentum. There he promptly bumped into a Rolls-Royce. The two drivers got out, and without much discussion,

Siffert gave him his business card with the message "We'll settle this later; I'm in a big hurry." Back in the car, the Formula 1 driver gave himself a thoughtful look before asking my father, "I think I know that man. Do you know who that was?" My father's answer came promptly: "Yes, of course: Udo Jürgens!" Jürgens was a well-known Austrian composer and singer.

Prost's Driving License

Unthinkable from today's point of view was my experience at Monza 1979, when Marc Surer in the BMW M1 ProCar in the Ascari variant stopped at the place where I was taking pictures and said to me

In all the years we photographed motorsport, we were chauffeured around by various drivers, from Wolfgang Count Berghe von Trips in a VW Beetle, to Clay Regazzoni in a Swiss mail truck, to Bernie Ecclestone in a Jeep.

after the end of the race, "Come on, get in." Since the car was no longer running, we were admittedly only towed. According to today's regulations, Marc would probably have received a five-race ban, and I would have lost my accreditation.

Another story happened in 1999 in the media parking lot at Spa-Francorchamps. There, I found a Swiss driver's license on the ground next to my car. I picked it up, opened it, and was immediately surprised. The license belonged to Alain Prost. Being an honest person, I immediately returned the document to him. However, I was sorely tempted to hand this special paper to the hand of the officer at the next police check.

On Criminal Paths

In 2011, a photo shoot with Simona de Silvestro in the Lamborghini Aventador almost ended in an arrest. Since there was fog in the Tösstal valley near Winterthur on this autumn day, I drove toward the sun with the Swiss racing driver. We finally arrived under a blue sky and began the shoot. First, we did the classic picture of her behind the wheel, driving. To gain more separation from my subject, I opened the scissor door on the passenger side and sat on the console. We drove slowly into a village. Simona laughed at a little boy on his bicycle, who frantically pedaled away from us. He jumped off his two-wheeler in front of a house and ran inside. Later, when we were taking pictures with the car stopped, a young woman came up to us and wanted to know exactly what we were doing. The driver of a post office vehicle also stopped beside us to see what we were doing. The scene became eerier and eerier until we were enlightened by another mother. There had been a case of child abuse just a few days earlier. Cautioned by their parents and teachers, the young people were on the alert. So the super sports car with the open passenger-side door did not fit into the usual picture of this small, idyllic village. Meanwhile, the boy was still holed up in the house, refusing to go to school in the afternoon out of fear. So we paid him a visit and cleared up the misunderstanding. In return, he was allowed to take a ride with Simona in the super sports car, which helped him overcome his fear.

Incidentally, De Silvestro took second place in Houston two years later, becoming the third woman after Sarah Fisher and Danica Patrick to score an Indy car podium finish.

Cross-Country with Schumacher

The cab rides with Klaus Ludwig in the DTM Mercedes or with Hans Stuck in the ProCar BMW M1 on the Nordschleife remain fond memories. Also unforgettable is my drive with Michael Schumacher in 1997 in the Fiat Abarth Trofeo on the Ferrari test track in Fiorano. The engine of the small junior car for rally racing produced just 55 hp, and the car weighed just under 800 kg (1,763 lbs.). Schumi was of course used to different dimensions. Suddenly he decided that it was not really a road-racing car and did not belong on an asphalt track. No sooner said than done—he turned off the track and drove off rally style, criss-crossing the meadow. Photos were, of course, no longer possible with all the jostling. Cruising through Monte Carlo with him in a Mercedes convertible in 1995 was a much more comfortable experience!

With Massa via São Paulo

On the Petronas tour in Malaysia in 2007 in beautiful Malacca, we were suddenly unable to find our bus driver. The entire party was waiting for him in the vehicle. So Robert Kubica got behind the wheel of a bus for the first time in his life and drove off slowly. But he didn't get far. It took only a few seconds before one of the passengers shouted that the driver was running behind us like a maniac.

Sometimes, I got invitations for great trips beyond the asphalt track. For example, I was able to spend a great afternoon with skipper Nelson Piquet off Fortaleza, driven by the wind on the waves of the Atlantic. And with Felipe Massa, there was an unforgettable sightseeing tour in a helicopter over the rooftops of São Paulo.

Marc Surer, Felipe Massa, Mark Webber,
and Mika Häkkinen

Nelson Piquet, Niki Lauda, Nelson Piquet,
and Robert Kubica

Jacques Villeneuve, Thierry Boutsen,
Jo Siffert, and Walter Röhrl

Simona de Silvestro, Sebastian Vettel, and Adrian Newey

28 Sleepless in Le Mans

Digitalization Turns Night into Day

Today, it's not out of the ordinary to take photos in the dark. In the days of analog photography, it was almost impossible to take nighttime photos of racing cars in motion, although there are a few excellent pit shots from Le Mans, Reims, Daytona, and Sebring. But these were possible only because the cars were motionless and the whole area was illuminated. Outstanding night action shots can be counted on one hand. In most of the pictures, only the two headlights of the cars stand out from the black surroundings.

Uncommonly Good Color Shots

Color films, with an ISO of 400, which could be pushed to ISO 800 with special development, were much less sensitive to light than black-and-white films. That's why color night shots are a true rarity. To make matters worse, lenses with a long focal length used to have a maximum lens speed of f4.0, often as low as f5.6.

In the 1960s, Kodak launched the 2475 Recording black-and-white film with a sensitivity of 1600 ASA (ISO). This was a quantum leap for that time. The 35mm format film was very coarse grained. On the other hand, the grain was drastically reduced by the medium-format camera, which was about four times larger. Now it was possible to take atmospheric night shots, especially in the pits, even without a tripod. From time to time, I was also able to get a shot of a passing car.

In 1964, my father took pictures at the 12-hour race at Reims. He managed to get some unique shots of the start using the Hasselblad 6x6 on a tripod with Kodak 2475 recording film. The race did not start in the afternoon in daylight as at Le Mans, but exactly at midnight, when it was completely dark. After the finish at noon on Sunday, the second highlight followed a short time later with the French Grand Prix. Sports cars and race cars were on the grid in Reims on the same weekend.

◀ Long exposure at the Carousel during the Nürburgring 24-hour race.

In the case of the Porsche 911 GT3 R, photographed in complete darkness, one can even make out the glow in the exhaust.

This panning shot of Felipe Massa's Williams in the Bahrain night race turns the spark points into long dashes, and the meager "Christmas lights" result in the blurry lighting effects above the car.

Fernando Alonso won the 2018 Le Mans 24 Hours in his first attempt in the Toyota TS050 with Buemi and Nakajima. After his two GP victories in Monaco (2006 and 2007), the only thing missing from his "triple crown" is success at the Indy 500, which he narrowly missed in 2017.

A nighttime dream shot from the analog period. Tony Adamowicz and Chuck Parsons's Ferrari 312P makes the raindrops dance with its headlights.

Like a silhouette, Esteban Gutiérrez
comes over the hill in the Sauber C32
in the Abu Dhabi twilight (2013).

Annoying Circular Saw

Today's digital cameras have almost no limits. Since light sensitivity can be increased almost to infinity, fantastic driving shots are possible even in very low light—even with long focal lengths. But all this technical progress also brings its disadvantages. Today, the xenon headlights on racing cars are extremely bright. In frontal shots, the eye and camera can no longer recognize the cars because of the glaring cone of light, and the autofocus veers off into the distance.

Digitization also changed the working hours of photographers. Shooting is now possible around the clock. Night becomes day. In the age of analog photography, photographers would capture only a few pit stops and nighttime impressions with light strips on film in the dark. After that, they could lie down in their cars in the press parking lot until dawn and sleep for a few hours. But here, too, there was an exception. At the 1991 Le Mans 24-hour race, the Mazda 787B driven by Johnny Herbert, Volker Weidler, and Bertrand Gachot completely deprived us of sleep. The car's rotary engine sounded like an unspeakably loud buzz saw and roused us from our sleep lap after lap. At least the car won the race, which gave the noise a certain legitimacy.

▲▲ This panning shot from the grandstand at Le Mans of the Porsche 956 flying down the start-finish straight in the dim backlight of the pit area was the height of emotion in the analog age.

▲ In 1999, the BMW V12 LMR surprisingly won the 24-hour classic at Le Mans. This night shot was taken with a slow shutter speed and a fill-in flash.

This picture of the brightly lit race-track in the heart of Singapore was taken from a room in the Swissotel.

Midnight in the Champagne region at the start of the 12 Hours of Reims 1964. The long exposure shot from a tripod allows the still-motionless cars to be clearly seen, while all that can be seen of the others is a ghost image (see-through) or even just streaks of light.

A long exposure, like this one taken at Le Mans (Esses), transforms the taillights into red stripes and reveals the ideal line taken by the cars.

Men and Myths:
Faces for Eternity

Enzo Ferrari (Feb. 18, 1898–Aug. 14, 1988) made himself into a myth. He built unique cars and pursued a clear brand strategy. His melodious name with the emblem of a prancing horse against a yellow background has been omnipresent in racing for decades. Whether in victory or defeat, the huge worldwide fan community always cheers or suffers along with Scuderia Ferrari. Ferrari is pure emotion!

Only a few people have met Enzo Ferrari personally. Nevertheless, all Ferrari fans know what he looked like during his lifetime. Numerous photos in books and magazines are responsible for this. They ensure that his face is imprinted in our memory.

Enzo Ferrari was rarely at the racetrack. Consequently, there is little visual material about the charismatic Italian. Photographer Julius Weitmann was one of the few who maintained a personal relationship with him. He succeeded in capturing unique moments in the life of Enzo Ferrari. My father had a very good connection with Sig at that time. Dottore Franco Gozzi, who had worked his way up from media delegate to sports director of Scuderia Ferrari, was considered a "shadow" of Enzo Ferrari. Through him, my father also learned about the Ferrari myth. Almost all the Ferrari yearbooks from the 1960s and 1970s contain pictures with the credit "Photo: Josef Reinhard, Sachseln." At the end of the year, my father always received a package with a yearbook, an exclusive leather-bound diary, and a business card with Ferrari's personal signature. As a special thank you for his photographic work, in 1966 he received an invitation to Maranello for an exclusive factory tour and lunch with the boss himself.

"When Your Own Wheel Passes You, You're in a Lotus"

Another myth arose in England around Lotus. Its founder was Anthony Colin Bruce Chapman (May 19, 1928–Dec. 16, 1982). Chapman was a technical genius. He revolutionized automobile racing with extreme lightweight construction and later the monocoque as well as the engine, which became the supporting element in his cars. Later, he set standards with the wedge shape of the Lotus 72, and also with the incorporation of aerodynamics from aircraft design in the groundbreaking winged cars that stuck to the ground. Not all of his innovations were successful. The turbine car, for example, announced with great anticipatory praise, failed miserably.

Colin Chapman's cars were a tightrope walk. The Briton pushed technology to the limit. For example, he said, "A race car has only one purpose: to win races. If it can't do that, it was a waste of time, money, and effort," or "A good race car is built to fall apart after the finish line." Graham Hill commented sarcastically, "When your own rear wheel passes you,

Handwritten card from Enzo Ferrari to my father from 1957

▶ Enzo Ferrari in conversation with his longtime press representative Sig. Dottore Franco Gozzi in the old paddock at Monza during the 1,000km race in 1970

Colin Chapman (May 19, 1928–Dec. 16, 1982) is considered one of the most ingenious racing car builders of all time. With the "wing car," he brought "upside-down" aircraft aerodynamics to automobile racing. What creates lift for an aircraft can also press a racing car onto the road.

then you know you're in a Lotus." And Jochen Rindt said of Chapman, "That's a man taking six people into an elevator that's only rated for three."

In 1960, Stirling Moss took the first victory for Colin Chapman's racing team in the small and light Lotus 18 in the Principality of Monaco. In total, Team Lotus won seventy-nine races. It won seven titles in the Constructors' World Championship and six in the Drivers' World Championship.

Faces for Eternity

Faces are imprinted in our brains and can be recalled again and again. Racing drivers Jo Siffert, Jochen Rindt, and Gilles Villeneuve are always present in our minds. Ayrton Senna died on May 1, 1994, more than twenty-five years ago. We still remember his face clearly. But how would he look today at the age of sixty? Such a conclusion is not an issue for us. A person who was torn from life at a young age remains in our memory at that age. Pictures that capture moments for eternity make sure of that.

Australian Jack Brabham (April 2, 1926–May 19, 2014) is to this day and very likely forever the only racing driver to become world champion (1966) in a race car he designed himself.

There was always a love-hate relationship between Jochen Rindt and Colin Chapman. The German-Austrian once said, "I will either become world champion with Lotus or I will die." Both came true in 1970, when he became world champion posthumously.

New Zealander Bruce McLaren founded McLaren, a company that is still in existence today. Only Ferrari is a little older, but even McLaren no longer builds only racing cars. Bruce McLaren had an accident too early to also win the F1 world championship in a car produced by his company, in addition to the CanAm championship.

In this picture, he is seen driving 1966 McLaren's first Formula 1 car, the M2B, through the streets of Monte Carlo.

Night Bivouac and Rain Gods

Many spectators long for rain races in Formula 1. For the drivers, it feels like driving on eggs in a car with up to 1,000 hp—and, of course, it's hoped that none of them are crushed. Breakdowns are inevitable. But we photographers also struggle in wet conditions. While the journalists enjoy coffee and cake in the dry media center, we stand unprotected beside the racetrack in the pouring rain and try to keep our photographic equipment dry. In the event of an interruption, any shelter is good enough for us. In Interlagos, I actually spent more than an hour in a smelly porta-potty for the track marshals, waiting patiently for the aborted practice session to resume. Anyone who thinks that normality would return to us in the evening is very much mistaken. Back in the hotel room, the chaos continued. All the equipment and clothes had to be dried for the next day. Usually, a hairdryer helped. In the past, when there was only a bed, a Bible, and a closet in the room, a hairdryer was part of our luggage just like a toothbrush. Hotels used to have bathrooms with tubs, but without showers, on each floor, but not in the rooms. One could consider oneself lucky to have a washbasin within one's own four walls.

At Spa-Francorchamps, when photographer Carl Imber was warming up his chilled, wet feet, one by one, of course, in warm water, the washbasin fell onto the floor. This guaranteed that there would be additional stress on departure.

Jean-Paul Belmondo

The 1984 Monaco Grand Prix went down in history as one of the most spectacular rain races ever. At first, the race organizers postponed the start by forty-five minutes because of the bad weather, but then they allowed the race to go ahead in pouring rain. On the thirty-first lap, race director Jacky Ickx stopped the race under pressure from leader Alain Prost in the McLaren-Tag Porsche. But the real heroes were Ayrton Senna in the Toleman-Hart and Stefan Bellof in the Tyrrell-Ford. If the race had gone the full distance, one of the two would have won.

◄ It's not easy to capture the "water rats" on film, but this image of Belgian driver Jacky Ickx in the Ferrari 512S with rain covering the windshield is almost perfect.

Raindrops created a silhouette of an F1 race car.

Heavy, dark thunderclouds with thunder and lightning announce the daily tropical rain in Malaysia in 2015. It is high time for the photographers to protect the cameras and themselves from the coming downpour.

When the race began, I was standing at the Mirabeau corner and was already completely soaked before the start. Halfway through the race, it became visibly more difficult to change film. The wetness permeated everything. Bent over in a protective posture, I tried to open the camera each time so that it wouldn't fill up with water. Then, miraculously, the rain stopped. When the new film was in and the lid closed, I straightened up and realized that the bad weather was still there. A man in a soaked white suit and loafers of the finest kind had stood next to me and held his umbrella over my head. I thanked him politely and realized that it was one of the very big celebrities who had helped me: actor Jean-Paul Belmondo.

To Sidney in My Underpants

The 1991 Australian rain race in Adelaide went down in history as the shortest F1 race with 14 laps, 53 kilometers (33 miles) or 25 minutes of racing. On the fifth lap, the two Benettons driven by Nelson Piquet and Michael Schumacher collided, and on the thirteenth, Mauricio Gugelmin slammed his Leyton House into the pit wall, injuring two track marshals. Then, when Mansell (Williams) and Berger (McLaren) also slid off the track, the race was stopped. At this point, I tried to get my two Nikon FM2 cameras, which had given up the ghost, going again under a pedestrian overpass. All of a sudden, the roar of the engines fell silent. A track marshal told me that the race had been stopped. I was not unhappy about this and wanted to get to the airport as quickly as possible. I had already checked my luggage for the return flight to Sydney early that morning. Due to the race cancellation, all the fans streamed off the track with me. It was impossible to get a cab. So I

However, the real heroes were Ayrton Senna in the Toleman Hart and Stefan Bellof in the Tyrrell Ford. If the race had gone the full distance, one of the two would have won.

looked for any ride. In the end, I hitched a ride in the open back of a pickup truck, and it got me to the airport just in time. I found myself standing at the check-in counter, soaked to the underpants. Changing clothes was out of the question because the suitcase with my dry clothes was already in the fuselage of the jet. But necessity is the mother of invention. In the air-conditioned aircraft, I stripped down to my underpants and wrapped myself in three wool blankets, in order to avoid developing hypothermia. But when I landed in Sydney, I had to get back into my wet clothes, which had been cooled down by the air conditioning, and could change in the toilet only after claiming my baggage. I disposed of the wet clothes at the airport.

Emergency Bivouac at Donington

In England, I experienced rain battles three times: in 1993, 2000, and 2012. On all three weekends, it poured almost without interruption. Everything was wet. The photographer's room looked terrible and reminded me of a Nepalese emergency bivouac on Mount Everest. In the hotel room, we turned the stoves up to maximum during the night, in an attempt to dry out our completely soaked clothes laid out all over the room. But the weather forecast predicted no improvement, and we had to fight our way from day to day. Motivation, energy, and temperature all dropped toward zero.

A favorite saying of mine is "The crappier the weather, the better the pictures." That may be justified in a thunderstorm of foreseeable duration, but with three days of constant rain and mud, such statements do not go down well with colleagues. Beside the track there was also an icy wind, which constantly blew the drizzle into our camera lenses. In order to get reasonably clear pictures, they had to be cleaned constantly. But with what, with all of our clothes soaked and nothing left that was dry?

Nevertheless, at Donington in 1993, the first of these three rain battles, we were treated to a highlight. Ayrton Senna started like the fire brigade in his inferior McLaren-Ford. His starting lap went down in history. He overtook Schumacher, Wendlinger, Hill, and Prost under the most difficult conditions and finished the first lap with the lead. In the end, he won the race in superior fashion.

If it doesn't rain naturally, then the track is watered. Sometimes a track is flooded for testing of rain tires. Niki Lauda on Ferrari's own wet track at Fiorano in 1973.

In the pouring rain of Spain, Michael Schumacher roars down the wet track in impressive fashion toward his first victory for Ferrari.

Finland's Mika Hakkinen in the
McLaren Mercedes makes the water
splash at the 1995 Argentine GP in
Buenos Aires.

Finnish driver Heikki Kovalainen in the
Caterham CT01 wallows in the grass
at Melbourne in 2012.

Ayrton Senna, one of the "rain gods," in
his element

1993 Brazilian Grand Prix: a heavy thundershower flooded the race-track within seconds. Cars crashed while driving on the straight. In the picture, Karl Wendlinger passes between the stranded cars of the two Japanese drivers Ukyo Katayama and Aguri Suzuki.

> Schumacher's victory was historic. Count Berghe von Trips had been the first German to win in a Ferrari. The joy among the tifosi (Ferrari supporters) was boundless.

By the time of the third English rain battle at Silverstone in 2012, I had already switched to digital photography. The digital cameras of the time were extremely sensitive to wet conditions, but they had one big advantage. In contrast to rolls of film, there were now so many shots available on a single memory card that there was no need to change them.

Schumacher's First Ferrari Victory

At the 1996 Spanish GP in Barcelona, Schumacher's star really rose at Ferrari. For the first time, the German took the lead in a Ferrari and proved his extra class on a wet track. Schumi made no mistake and won the race with a commanding forty-five-second lead. He had the fastest race lap, and it was no less than 2.2 seconds faster than the second-fastest time. Schumacher's victory was historic. Before that, Count Berghe von Trips had been the only German driver to manage a win in a Ferrari. The joy among the tifosi was boundless. For me, the most important thing was to have a picture of the victory ceremony. But then, at the decisive moment, my rain-soaked camera began to act up. When I took the first shot, it immediately exposed the entire film and rewound it as well.

I needed two pictures: one of the trophy being lifted and one of the champagne spraying. Spontaneously, only one possibility came to mind: open the camera back, put in the film, wait until Michael lifted the trophy, then close the back and hold it down. I repeated the same process with the champagne shower. It worked and I had my pictures.

A dark night for the start of the Japanese Grand Prix at Suzuka on November 6, 1994. Still in the days of analog technology, we photographers really reached the limits of our equipment here. Shutter speeds of 1/125th of a second at full aperture and film pushed to 200 ASA were the highest of highs.

Ayrton Senna and Michael Schumacher were probably the two best "water rats." When it got wet, they were even faster and remained absolutely flawless.

Their car control was always a feast for the eyes. How do you depict these two drivers as rain gods? The picture of Michael Schumacher was taken during his Mercedes days (1991), entirely by chance during a fitness training session in Austria, and I captured Ayrton Senna after a thundershower at the French GP in Magny-Cours (1992) through the wet flap of the McLaren motorhome.

Photographing Formula 1 Engines–Now Strictly Forbidden

Engines are the heart of the race car. In the early days of racing, they were hidden under the front hood, then later they were uncovered as a supporting element in the middle of the car, and today they are completely hidden again. Many technology freaks have given motorsport the cold shoulder in recent years because the teams have declared the inner workings of their cars to be a big secret and are unwilling to reveal so much as a screw.

The Most Successful

The most successful engine in F1 history is the 3-liter (183-cubic inch) Ford-Cosworth DFV V8. It was first used in 1967 at Zandvoort in the Lotus 49 driven by Jim Clark and Graham Hill. Clark immediately won the first victory by a car powered by the new engine. Until 1983, the engine was partly responsible for winning 155 races, twelve drivers' titles, and ten constructors' titles. My father experienced his baptism of fire with the Hasselblad in Holland. Seventeen years later, with the Pentax 6 × 7, I photographed the final evolution of the engine, the DFY, in the Tyrrell driven by Michele Alboreto.

The most successful F1 engine, the Ford Cosworth DFV, made its debut in the Lotus 49 of Jim Clark and Graham Hill at the 1967 Dutch Grand Prix. Hill took the pole position, and Clark won the race.

just the test bench; no, the entire company was without power. This was, of course, embarrassing for the employees who were present. When the excitement had died down, the fuses were changed. To prevent a second short circuit, I was required to draw power from a distant outbuilding via several extension cords.

The Craziest

My father and I experienced many engines. Not all of them were successful. Some never even made it to the racetrack. The craziest chapter was written by Guy Nègre. In 1990, the French engine designer wanted to revolutionize Formula 1 with a completely new concept. He built a 12-cylinder engine with the cylinders in a W configuration. The special thing about it was that the engine was to get by without valves. Roller slide valves were provided for gas exchange. In 1989, we visited Nègre for Sport-Auto in a small village in Provence. When he and his twelve-man team fired up the W12 on the test bench, we felt as if we were in a Louis de Funès (a French actor and comedian) movie. It all resembled a gigantic handcraft project, and the cooling-water supply reminded me of the Disney cartoon character Gyro Gearloose. The water came via a garden hose from the washbasin in the toilet located near the test stand. After running at low revs for just a short time, the engine began to screech and steam and gave the impression that it was about to fly apart. Before it got that far, Nègre turned off the power.

Incidentally, the engine never made it into a racing car and the promised revolution failed to materialize.

Mortal Danger

Unlike Guy Nègre, the factories put the engines through their paces professionally. The units are trimmed to maximum rpm under the greatest safety precautions until all the exhaust manifolds glow bright red. This visually impressive spectacle is not easy to capture on film. It is strictly forbidden to be in the test bench area during a test. If an engine explodes, the flying parts punch fist-sized holes in the concrete walls. You can't imagine what would happen to a photographer in such a situation. In addition, the high speed of the engine creates such severe vibrations that any camera, even on a heavy tripod, begins to move.

Mario Illien from Chur is by far the most successful engine builder in racing. In this picture, he is seen with his daughter Noel, who actively supports him in his design work.

Lights Out

My assignment as photographer in 1988 at Alfa Corse, the Alfa Romeo factory racing team, in Milan was a special experience. I wanted to photograph technical director Giuseppe Tonti with the V10 engine, which was intended for the Alfa Romeo 164 Silhouette ProCar, in the test bench. As I was trying to shed some light with my studio flashes, something unbelievable happened. After I fired the first test flash, there was a loud bang and all the lights went out. Not

Lights out at Autodelta. A single test flash in the engine test facility was enough to paralyze the entire company.

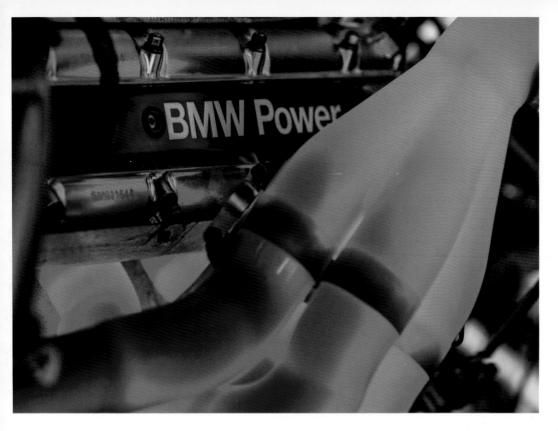

The engines are put through their paces on the test benches and made to glow. Thanks to digital technology, the images can be checked immediately.

When I was asked to photograph the C9 Sauber Group C engine on the test bench at Mercedes in 1988, I had not the slightest idea of all this. Completely perplexed, I stood there when I was told that I was not allowed to take pictures in the test bench area. So there was no picture to be taken without a remote shutter release. Or was there? There was a way—the engineers revved up the engine, made the turbocharger and manifold glow, and then shut down the engine. At that exact moment, I opened the door, ran into the room, and took two or three pictures before everything had cooled down again.

Of course, these were not optimal conditions. But I saw it as the only way to take photos. Later at BMW Sauber, equipped with a remote release and digital camera, everything was easier. Whereas in analog photography the lighting conditions from the studio flash and the glow were still very difficult to assess, now with the digital camera the pictures could be viewed immediately and the settings changed if necessary.

The Last One

Ferrari hung on to twelve-cylinder engines for a long time, even when it had long been clear to everyone that ten-cylinder engines were more effective. In 1995 in Adelaide, the time had come. Ferrari used a 12-cylinder engine for the last time in the 412T2 driven by Gerhard Berger and Jean Alesi. I covered Berger's last 12-cylinder drive for Austrian Auto Revue. For once, the traditional Italian racing team made possible something that was actually strictly forbidden. I was officially allowed to photograph in the Ferrari pit as the very last 12-cylinder engine was installed in the car before the race. A short time later, the 12-cylinder era was history.

Gerhard Berger still remembers well the farewell to the power units of the time. "You'll never hear a sound like that again," he said to himself during the race. Today, there is one of those V12 engines in his office in Wörgl.

By the way, it's currently unthinkable to photograph an engine change. Even later as an official Sauber-Ferrari photographer, I was forbidden by Maranello to take pictures with the hood removed and the engine visible.

Though strictly forbidden, the Italian traditional racing team made it possible for once. I was officially allowed to take pictures in the Ferrari pit . . .

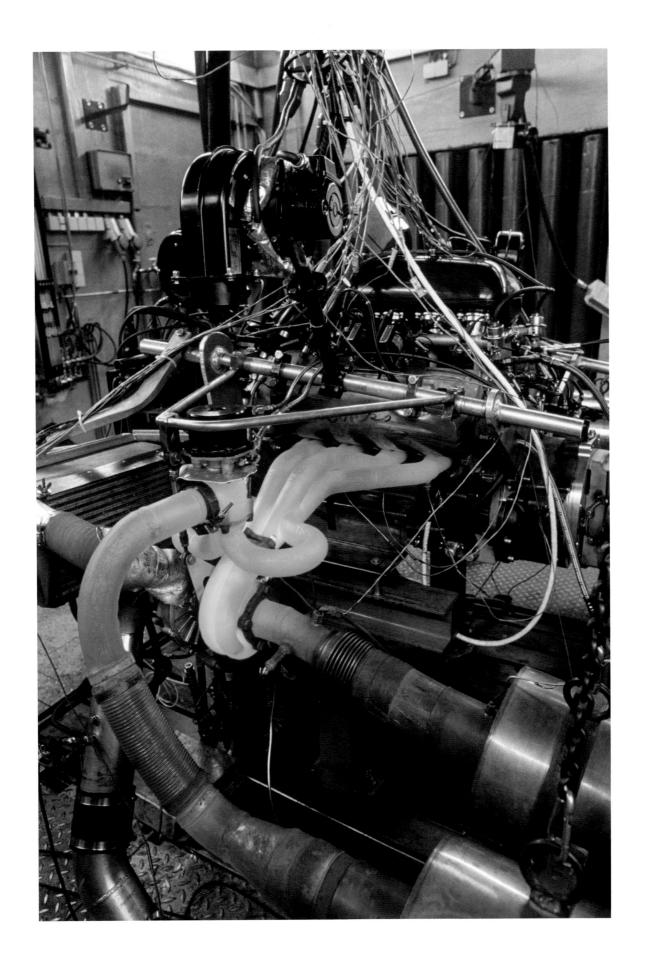

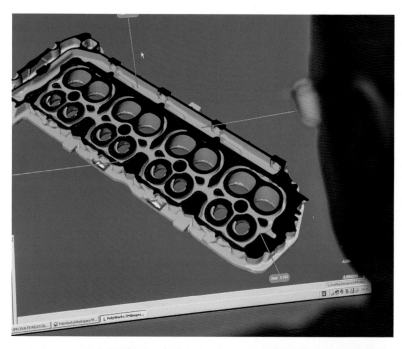

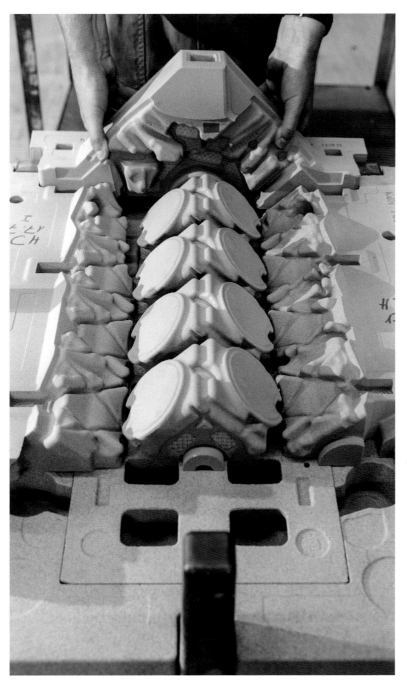

A few very deep glimpses into that which is hidden. The year 2007 in BMW's engine foundry in Landshut, where not only production engines but the F1 power units as well were built.

When F1 cars were still really loud, they impressed everyone. At the BMW Christmas party in Seefeld, for example, music was made without a DJ.

◀ The Pratt & Whitney turbine of the Lotus 56B. The car, which was much too heavy, with extremely poor responsiveness (and still equipped with all-wheel drive), started only three races. Dave Walker drove it in Holland, Reine Wisell in England, and Emerson Fittipaldi at Monza. Only in Italy did the car take the checkered flag.

31 Suzuka for First and Second

When One Could Still Become World Champion Despite a Crash

The first opponent is always one's own teammate, so it's not unusual for the two to get in each other's way. At the 1975 Spanish GP at Montjuïc, both Ferraris were in the front row. Niki Lauda maintained his pole position at the start ahead of Clay Regazzoni. Mario Andretti got into a tangle with Vittorio Brambilla before the hairpin and in the turmoil touched Lauda's Ferrari, which then flew into the guardrail together with his teammate, of all people. In the end, the Austrian took the world championship despite this unfortunate incident.

A Crash Helps Prost

The great cockfight between the two McLaren drivers Ayrton Senna and Alain Prost reached its first climax on October 22, 1989, at the Japanese Grand Prix. Prost took the lead after the start and extended it to 4.6 seconds after the pit stop. The Frenchman was determined to finish ahead of Senna so as not to postpone the title fight to Adelaide. But then Senna made up ground and closed the gap with his teammate. When braking for the narrow chicane near the pit lane entrance, the leader left the inside lane open for a moment. The Brazilian immediately attempted to pass. But Prost refused to give way in the tight

duel and closed the door. The two McLaren cars tangled and came to a halt in the emergency exit of the chicane. Prost got out of the car and abandoned the race. But Senna gestured wildly to the track marshals and let them push him. He then drove the laps of his life and actually went on to win the race. Later, however, he was disqualified by the FIA president, Frenchman Jean-Marie Balestre, and the stewards for shortcutting the chicane. Prost thus became world champion.

I was standing on the photo podium of the chicane at the time and realized that Senna was getting closer and closer to his teammate, who was in the

◀ Teammates in close quarters. Lauda is pushed into teammate Regazzoni by Andretti before the first corner at the Spanish Grand Prix. They said goodbye to one another at the guardrails.

FIA president Jean-Marie Balestre did everything he could to make his compatriot Alain Prost the world champion at Suzuka in 1989.

Two world championship decisions involving Senna and Prost took place in Japan. The pair were teammates at McLaren, and the Frenchman won the title with the help of the FIA. A year later, there was another crash between the two drivers—but this time prompted by the Brazilian, who had to start on the worse line despite having the pole position: "If Prost goes into the first corner in front of me, I'll shoot him down." No sooner said than done!

lead. I was also aware that the title was at stake. On top of that, braking into the chicane is the best passing opportunity at Suzuka. So I decided to remain where I was and, if necessary, miss the podium ceremony rather than this all-decisive duel. And lo and behold, only a short time later there was a crash. Admittedly, the first picture with the slightly elevated Senna next to Prost was blurred. But then I was able to capture the rest of the action absolutely perfectly. So I had the world championship decision in the can.

A Crash Helps Senna

A year later, the starting position was the same, but with the positions reversed—Senna was ahead of Prost, who had since switched to Ferrari, in the world championship standings. Before the race, Senna warned that he would drive into Prost's car if the latter turned into the first corner in the lead.

No one wanted to believe what he had said. Nevertheless, we were in the first corner at the start. And sure enough, there was a crash right before our eyes. Knowing that there would likely be a crash did not make it easy for me to select the focal length. Long with close cropping, or short with an overview? I opted for the long version and thus had only half of the accident that happened directly in front of me in the picture. Later, I photographed Senna and Prost climbing over the guardrail independently of one another on their way back to the pits. "Bretti," our longtime layout artist at *Sport Auto*, cleverly put the two pictures together on a double page, taking advantage of the gap in the binding in the center of the magazine, so that everyone believed the two had climbed over the guardrail close together and at the same time. By the way, this time Senna secured the world championship title.

Who is stronger? The two fighting cocks (Prost on the left, Senna on the right) on the scales.

32 The Last Check

Risk Rides with the Driver

Motorsport is, or rather was, extremely dangerous! Helmut Zwickl aptly described the period from the 1950s to the 1980s: "Back when sex was safe, but F1 was dangerous . . ." Jo Siffert said, "Every person receives a checkbook at birth. Every time he has been really lucky in life, he loses a check. Unfortunately, nobody knows how many checks there are in his checkbook." And Jochen Rindt said, "Every day brings us closer to the end, only no one knows how many more there will be!"

Death has been with us all these years. We have witnessed some of the most serious accidents up close and were forced to watch as great eras came to an end. These include the fatal events that took the lives of Count Berghe von Trips at Monza on September 10, 1961; Lorenzo Bandini at Monaco on May 7, 1967; Jim Clark at Hockenheim on April 7, 1968; Piers Courage on June 21, 1970; Roger Williamson at Zandvoort on July 29, 1973; Jochen Rindt on September 5, 1970; Ronnie Peterson on September 11, 1978, at Monza; Markus Höttinger on April 13, 1980, at Hockenheim; Gilles Villeneuve on May 8, 1982, at Zolder; and Roland Ratzenberger and Ayrton Senna on the black race weekend of April 30 and May 1, 1994, at Imola. Trips would probably have become the first German world champion, Jim Clark could have become the most successful racing driver ever, Rindt did not even live to see his own world championship title, and who knows how the further duels between Michael Schumacher and Ayrton Senna would have turned out?

Each accident wrote its own story—for us photographers, too.

Jim Clark, Hockenheim, 1968

The pictures of Jim Clark's accident scene are extremely rare contemporary documents. Only two photographers arrived on the scene shortly after the crash, Werner Eisele and my father. Eisele's bad luck was that he was the first to arrive at the scene of the accident. The photos he took were seized shortly afterward by Huschke von Hanstein for use in the accident investigation. Thus, Eisele came away pretty empty-handed. The film was never returned, despite promises to the contrary. My father was luckier. He was able to bring home the footage of the wrecked Lotus. Thanks to the Hasselblad with its interchangeable magazines, he was even able to take a few color slides in addition to the black-and-white shots. The pictures went around the world and were again in great demand in 2018, fifty years after the accident. My dad was very focused on the Scotsman that weekend and began photographing the racing in the Motodrom, but when he heard about a serious accident shortly after the start and seeing Jim Clark missing from the field, he left the race to fight his way through the woods toward the east turn, where the accident site was located about 2 kilometers (1.24 miles) away. Meanwhile, the race continued, and Frenchman Jean Pierre Beltoise (Matra) won the first heat. Henri Pescarolo recalled, "We passed the

It was a long way for my father from the Motodrom to the East Curve to take a few sad images of Scottish driver Jim Clark's completely wrecked Lotus F2 after his fatal accident at Hockenheim in 1968.

Swedish driver Ronnie Peterson suffered worst in the fireball at the end of the narrowing start-finish straight at Monza. One day later, he died in the hospital, not from the accident injuries but from a pulmonary embolism.

▶+▲ Markus Höttinger's Maurer F2 was hardly damaged; only the roll bar was snapped off. The cause of death was a wheel from Derek Warwick's car, which struck him in the head.

▶ Fatal accident involving Axel Perrenoud during the Ollon-Villars hill climb in 1967. His Cobra left the track and ended up striking a barn.

accident site lap after lap, but we didn't know what had happened, certainly not that it was Clark." The latter was considered the fastest driver in the field at the time. Jackie Stewart put it in a nutshell after the fatal accident: "If it happens to the best of us, then who is safe?"

Ronnie Peterson, Monza, 1978

The accident occurred just a few meters after the start on the narrowing straightaway. Riccardo Patrese (Arrows Ford) pushed to the left and nudged James Hunt. His McLaren-Ford touched the rear wheel of the Swede driving next to him. The result was a mass collision, which hit the innocent Ronnie Peterson

the hardest. He survived the accident conscious, but with severe leg injuries. The following day he died of a pulmonary embolism in the hospital during emergency surgery.

Many of the photographers, my father included, were standing behind the guardrail of the first chicane at the start of the race and had the braking point in focus. Suddenly, a huge fireball spread in the background. Now it was a matter of keeping one's nerve and first taking the start picture with the few remaining cars. When they had passed the chicane, the photographers ran toward the scene of the accident. In all the commotion, a camera with a telephoto lens was stolen from my father's photo bag. Professional colleague Carl Imber had mounted a camera high on the fence, waiting with a long release cable from a distance for its release. But shocked by the accident, Kaspar Arnet, the man designated to release the shutter, forgot to operate it. So, unfortunately, the film remained blank.

Markus Höttinger, Hockenheimring, 1980

I photographed the start of the Formula 2 race from the grandstand. On the third lap, the cars driven by the Italian Andrea de Cesaris and the Englishman Derek Warwick touched each other. Both flew out of the first corner. The right rear wheel of Warwick's Toleman came off as a result of the accident. It flew about 15 meters (49 feet) into the air and then fell on the head of the unsuspecting Markus Höttinger, passing in the Maurer. The Austrian was killed on the spot. His car came to a stop on the right-hand side of the track just a few hundred meters after the turn. Without knowing what had really happened, I set off in the direction of Höttinger's car. When the race was stopped and the ambulance roared up, I ran to the scene of the accident. I saw efforts being made to resuscitate the young driver. Later, he was flown away by helicopter. Unknowingly, I also took a picture of the roll bar, which was half cut off. It wasn't until hours later that I learned the true circumstances of the accident.

Gilles Villeneuve, Zolder, 1982

Zolder was my first race of the season at that time, since I had no customers for the previous overseas races. The year before, Gilles Villeneuve had complained to me at Monza that I only ever brought Jody Scheckter chocolate, but that he loved it, too. So I surprised Villeneuve in Zolder with some of the best Swiss chocolate. He was so pleased that he spontaneously invited me to lunch.

The catering was still very modest at that time. The Ferrari motorhome was a converted coach with a table for about five people. There I sat on Saturday afternoon shortly before the start of qualifying, together with Gilles Villeneuve, and enjoyed a plate of pasta from Ferrari's kitchen.

I immediately sensed that the chemistry between us was right and that a friendship could develop. Then Gilles Villeneuve went to his car and I went to my

Canadian driver Gilles Villeneuve had to hand in his last check at Zolder in 1982.

▶ Help came too late for Ayrton Senna at Imola on May 1, 1994.

photo location, the hill just after the chicane. Practice was underway, and I photographed the F1 cars on their laps. In his second and final attempt to take the pole, Villeneuve ran into the slow-moving RAM March driven by Jochen Mass. A misunderstanding between the two led to the collision. I heard a strange, dull thump behind me, turned around, but couldn't see anything as a result of the left-hand bend. Rally racing journalist Achim Schlang was standing next to me and just said that the two must have collided.

We ran off and saw the Canadian's badly battered Ferrari from a distance. After the contact with March, the car had become airborne and rolled over several times. Villeneuve was catapulted out of the car still in his seat, thrown across the track, and struck a post of the safety fence. Not only was my grief at the Canadian's death immense, but the entire Formula 1 fan community lost an idol in the form of the popular and daredevil Ferrari star.

Ayrton Senna and Roland Ratzenberger, Imola, 1994

The absolute horror weekend of my 550-plus Grand Pris race career was the San Marino F1 at Imola on May 1, 1994. Helmut Zwickl summed it up: "The day the sun fell from the sky!" First, in the first qualifying session, Rubens Barrichello crashed in the Jordan and broke his arm. Then in the final qualifying session, Austrian Roland Ratzenberger flew off the track in the Simtec and died on the spot. On race day, Pedro Lamy hit JJ Lehto, who had stopped in front of him, at high speed at the start, leading to a safety car period. After the restart, Ayrton Senna, in the lead, crashed his Williams straight into the wall at the Tamburello corner. The cause was probably a broken steering column. On impact, a piece of the suspension of the broken wheel rammed through his helmet and into his head, inflicting the fatal injuries.

At the same time, I was standing in the Tosa curve, just under a kilometer away from the scene of the action. Over the track loudspeaker came the news of Senna's accident in the Tamburello. Knowing that this curve was a dangerous one, it was clear to me that the accident could have serious consequences. But the roads in Imola are long for photographers. Moreover, it's not possible to follow the track there either. To be flexible, I always had a folding bike with me at Imola. So I cycled off immediately. As one of the first on-site, I stood right at the fence opposite the smashed Williams. Senna was still sitting in the car. But before I was ready to take pictures, two policemen grabbed me and hauled me away, together with my equipment. Since I was authorized to take pictures, an intense discussion began, and they didn't know what to do with me. Since in the meantime hundreds of onlookers had flocked to the fence, the policemen let me go. But now I was too far away from the fence, and with my short stature I had no chance of seeing over the other heads, let alone take pictures. I took all the money out of my pocket and asked a tall, powerful-looking Italian to hoist me onto his shoulders with my 400mm lens. From this position, I took the pictures of Senna, who had of course long since been removed from the car and carried into the rescue helicopter.

Why do people photograph such scenes? In the moment of the moment, one has no idea what's going on. If one is "lucky" enough to capture a car becoming airborne, one mindlessly keeps the camera on the action for as long as possible. At that moment, one doesn't even begin to think that something could happen to the driver. Let's take the example of Robert

Kubica's freakish crash at the 2007 Canadian Grand Pris, when the BMW Sauber disintegrated upon hitting the wall. It was an accident of the worst kind. Everyone thought that the driver would certainly not get out. But Robert escaped with a concussion and a few bruises.

If the photographer, who was standing perfectly, had not taken a picture out of sheer reverence, it would have been a big mistake. With Jim Clark, it was quite different. One knew right away that he could never survive the crash. But the photographs are of documentary value in reconstructing the possible course of the accident. Moreover, officially in motorsports, no driver ever dies at the scene of the accident, because the whole procedure with the public prosecutor's office would bring the entire event to a standstill. It's "customary" that drivers die, at the earliest, in the helicopter or ambulance on the way to the hospital.

But the photographer should always check his pictures afterward. Showing the wrecked car is fine, but the bloody, seriously injured, or even dead driver does not have to be shown to the public. Italian photographer Angelo Orsi was standing on the TV tower at the time of Senna's accident and had a clear view of the scene where Ayrton was being treated next to the car. He took photos of it but never published them.

It is "customary" that drivers die, at the earliest, in the helicopter or ambulance on the way to the hospital.

Lotus lost two of its top drivers, Jochen Rindt and Ronnie Peterson, at Monza. The picture shows the Swede's completely wrecked Lotus being taken away.

When Jo Siffert was killed in an accident at Brands-Hatch at 2:18 p.m. on October 24, 1971, the clocks stopped all over Switzerland. Five days later, 50,000 people traveled to Freiburg to attend his funeral. Our country had never before experienced such a large funeral service. Swiss television broadcast the funeral live, and Siffert was posthumously named Swiss Sportsman of the Year.

▶ Fifty years later, on the anniversary of his death, a good five hundred fans once again made a pilgrimage to his final resting place at the St-Léonard cemetery in Freiburg for a minute's silence. More stories about Jo Siffert, Michael Schumacher, and Bernie Ecclestone, and many other topics, are still waiting to be told.

Racing is a game of perspective; only a few centimeters separate the cars from the red-and-white surfaces. With that small difference, the lateral curbs can become a rearing Cobra. In Austin, Texas, in 2013, Sebastian Vettel in the Red Bull RB9 took the pole position, set the fastest race lap, and also won the race.

About the Author

Daniel Reinhard's great photographic passion is car racing and vintage vehicles. His father Sepp ("Disaster Sepp") Reinhard and his grandfather Joseph Reinhard were both professional photographers.

In 1979, Daniel Reinhard, born in Sachseln, Switzerland, in 1960, took over the "job" of Formula 1 photographer from his father, and since then he has accompanied the drivers and their vehicles on race tracks all over the world. In the process, friendships developed with many people from the world of racing. This gave him insights and photographic opportunities that make his documentary and aesthetic behind-the-scenes views so unique.

His photographs have appeared and continue to appear not only in magazines such as *Auto, Motor und Sport*, and *Sport Auto*. Whenever exciting photos are needed, daily newspapers such as the *Swiss NZZ* (*Swiss Daily News*) also like to draw on the great photographic treasure trove of the Reinhard dynasty of photographers.

Together with Richard Kaan, Daniel Reinhard published the large-format illustrated book *Passion Oldtimer* in 2018.

For the five hundredth F1 Grand Prix I photographed (in Monza in 2010), I received great praise from Bernie Ecclestone, and Michael Schumacher also took the opportunity to congratulate me. Keep fighting, Michael!

OTHER SCHIFFER BOOKS ON RELATED SUBJECTS:
Air & Water: Rare Porsches, 1956–2019, curated by Stephen Struss, ISBN 978-0-7643-6416-7
Mythical Formula One: 1966 to Present, Marcel Correa, ISBN 978-0-7643-4581-4
Mercedes-Benz Supercars: From 1901 to Today, Thomas Wirth, ISBN 978-0-7643-4090-1

Originally published as *Inside Formel 1* ©2022, GeraMond Media GmbH, Munich. Translated from the German by Daniel Johnston.

Library of Congress Control Number: 2023931245

Cover design by Chris Bower
Production Design by Jack Chappell
Type set in Changeling NEO/Intro/Minion

ISBN: 978-0-7643-6679-6
Printed in China

Published by Schiffer Publishing, Ltd.
4880 Lower Valley Road
Atglen, PA 19310
Phone: (610) 593-1777; Fax: (610) 593-2002
Email: Info@schifferbooks.com
Web: www.schifferbooks.com

For our complete selection of fine books on this and related subjects, please visit our website at www.schifferbooks.com. You may also write for a free catalog.

Schiffer Publishing's titles are available at special discounts for bulk purchases for sales promotions or premiums. Special editions, including personalized covers, corporate imprints, and excerpts, can be created in large quantities for special needs. For more information, contact the publisher.

We are always looking for people to write books on new and related subjects. If you have an idea for a book, please contact us at proposals@schifferbooks.com.